I0419418

Editor-in-Chief and Founder:
    Lyndon H. LaRouche, Jr.
Editorial Board: *Lyndon H. LaRouche, Jr. , Helga
    Zepp-LaRouche, Paul Gallagher, Tony Papert,
    Gerald Rose, Dennis Small, Jeffrey Steinberg,
    William Wertz*
Co-Editors: *Paul Gallagher, Tony Papert*
Managing Editor: *Nancy Spannaus*
Technology: *Marsha Freeman*
Books: *Katherine Notley*
Ebooks: *Richard Burden*
Graphics: *Alan Yue*
Photos: *Stuart Lewis*
Circulation Manager: *Stanley Ezrol*

INTELLIGENCE DIRECTORS
Counterintelligence: *Jeffrey Steinberg, Michele
    Steinberg*
Economics: *John Hoefle, Marcia Merry Baker,
    Paul Gallagher*
History: *Anton Chaitkin*
Ibero-America: *Dennis Small*
Russia and Eastern Europe: *Rachel Douglas*
United States: *Debra Freeman*

INTERNATIONAL BUREAUS
Bogotá: *Miriam Redondo*
Berlin: *Rainer Apel*
Copenhagen: *Tom Gillesberg*
Houston: *Harley Schlanger*
Lima: *Sara Madueño*
Melbourne: *Robert Barwick*
Mexico City: *Gerardo Castilleja Chávez*
New Delhi: *Ramtanu Maitra*
Paris: *Christine Bierre*
Stockholm: *Ulf Sandmark*
United Nations, N.Y.C.: *Leni Rubinstein*
Washington, D.C.: *William Jones*
Wiesbaden: *Göran Haglund*

ON THE WEB
e-mail: eirns@larouchepub.com
www.larouchepub.com
www.executiveintelligencereview.com
www.larouchepub.com/eiw
Webmaster: *John Sigerson*
Assistant Webmaster: *George Hollis*
Editor, Arabic-language edition: *Hussein Askary*

EIR (ISSN 0273-6314) *is published weekly
(50 issues), by EIR News Service, Inc.,
P.O. Box 17390, Washington, D.C. 20041-0390.
(703) 777-9451*

European Headquarters: E.I.R. GmbH, Postfach
Bahnstrasse 9a, D-65205, Wiesbaden, Germany
Tel: 49-611-73650
Homepage: http://www.eirna.com
e-mail: eirna@eirna.com
Director: Georg Neudecker

Montreal, Canada: 514-461-1557

Denmark: EIR - Danmark, Sankt Knuds Vej 11,
basement left, DK-1903 Frederiksberg, Denmark.
Tel.: +45 35 43 60 40, Fax: +45 35 43 87 57. e-mail:
eirdk@hotmail.com.

Mexico City: EIR, Sor Juana Inés de la Cruz 242-2
Col. Agricultura C.P. 11360
Delegación M. Hidalgo, México D.F.
Tel. (5525) 5318-2301
eirmexico@gmail.com

Copyright: ©2015 EIR News Service. All rights
reserved. Reproduction in whole or in part without
permission strictly prohibited.

Canada Post Publication Sales Agreement
#40683579

Postmaster: Send all address changes to *EIR*, P.O.
Box 17390, Washington, D.C. 20041-0390.

Signed articles in *EIR* represent the views of the
authors, and not necessarily those of the Editorial
Board.

The Current Presidential Transition Period

About this Issue

In the current phase of his decades-old work in shaping the institution of the Presidency, Lyndon LaRouche is not only weaving together the institution of the next Presidency for after the scheduled 2016 elections,—for which Martin O'Malley is *so far* the only qualified prospective candidate on the horizon. Much more immediately, Obama's hand must be removed from the nuclear button now, if a likely war of nuclear extermination is to be avoided long before that next scheduled Presidential election. A transitional Presidency must begin to wield power immediately now. This issue of *EIR* is devoted to developing and elaborating the principles for that transition, as Lyndon LaRouche has pointed to them in organizing it.

EIR Contents

www.larouchepub.com   Volume 42, Number 23, June 5, 2015

Cover This Week

The Oval Office, October 2007

cc/Silver Starre

Martin O'Malley and the Institution of the Presidency

by Debra Hanania Freeman

June 1—On Saturday, May 30, former two-term Baltimore Mayor and Maryland Governor Martin O'Malley made his candidacy for the Democratic Presidential nomination official. Writing for Bloomberg News, Mark Halperin noted that the speech could very well serve as a "game changer" in the 2016 Presidential campaign.

O'Malley delivered his remarks standing atop Federal Hill, historic as a lookout post both during the War of 1812 and for Union troops during the Civil War. During better economic times, it also overlooked what was once a vibrant industrial port—a point that did not go unnoticed in O'Malley's remarks.

Although he addressed issues that ranged from the need for a new national security policy to immigration reform, O'Malley's emphasis remained consistent with what it has been from the start: the need to rebuild America's real economy. He didn't hesitate to address the recent riots that swept Baltimore following the death of Freddie Grey, but refused to reduce the issue, as so many so-called progressives have, to solely a racial one, saying:

> What took place here was not only about race... not only about policing in America. It's about

Martin O'Malley at his kickoff rally in Baltimore, May 30, 2015

everything it is supposed to mean to be an American. The scourge of hopelessness that happened to ignite here that evening, transcends race or geography. Witness the record numbers of young white kids killing themselves with heroin in suburbs and small towns across America.

And, while Hillary Clinton has refused to criticize Obama, O'Malley made no excuses for Obama:

> The hard truth of our shared reality is this: Unemployment in many American cities and in many small towns across the United States is higher now than it was eight years ago. The vast majority of the American people are poorer than they were eight years ago. And it isn't getting

better. It is getting worse. We can't run away from the truth. Conditions of extreme and growing poverty, create conditions for extreme violence. We have work to do....

Naming the Enemy

O'Malley laid the blame squarely on the dominance of Wall Street:

Our economic and political system is upside down and backwards, and it is time to turn it around. What happened to our economy,—what happened to the American Dream,—did not happen by chance. Nor was it merely the result of global forces somehow beyond our control. Powerful, wealthy special interests here at home have used our government to create—in our own country—an economy that is leaving a majority of our people behind. An economy that has so concentrated wealth in the hands of the very few, that it has taken opportunity from the homes of the many. An economy where a majority of our people are unheard, unseen, unneeded, and left to conclude that their lives and labors are literally worth less today than they were yesterday.... And will be worth less still tomorrow....

We are allowing our land of opportunity to be turned into a land of inequality. Main Street struggles, while Wall Street soars. Tell me how it is, that not a single Wall Street CEO was convicted of a crime related to the 2008 economic meltdown. *Not. A. Single. One.* Tell me how it is, that you can get pulled over for a broken tail light in our country, but if you wreck the nation's economy, you are untouchable.

This is not how our economy is supposed to work! This is not how our country is supposed to work! This is not the American Dream! And it does not have to be this way!

The presentation went beyond platitudes. He identified that the real substance of what is so commonly referred to as the American Dream, is the commitment to progress and to the future, above all else, stressing that before one can craft a solution to a problem, one has to understand the problem and its cause.

Our economy isn't based on money; our economy is people,—all of our people. The American system measures success by progress; by the growing prosperity, productivity, and security of our people,— all of our people.

We must put our national interest first, and that means putting the general welfare of the vast majority of our people first. But we cannot rebuild the American Dream here at home, by catering to the voices of the privileged and the powerful.

Look: It is high time that we were honest. They were the ones who turned our economy upside-down in the first place. And they are the only ones who are benefiting from it. Yes, we need to prosecute cheats, but we also need to act pre-emptively to restore stability to our banking system. How do we do that? There is ***no way around it!*** We need to reinstate Glass-Steagall, and we need to do that immediately. If a bank is too big to fail without wrecking our nation's economy, ... then it needs to be broken up before it breaks us ... again.

By the time O'Malley started naming names, the crowd's enthusiasm had reached a fever pitch. The candidate paused for the extended ovation before saying:

Listen, let me tell you a true story. I think most people know that Goldman Sachs is one of the biggest repeat-offending investment banks in America. Recently, back in March, Lloyd Blankfein, the CEO of Goldman Sachs, let his employees know that, as far as Wall Street reform is concerned, he'd be just fine with either Jeb Bush or Hillary Clinton.

Oh, I bet he would.... My friends, that should really tell us something.

"Well, I've got news for Mr. Blankfein and the bullies of Wall Street: The Presidency is not a crown to be passed back and forth by you and your friends between two royal families. It is a sacred trust to be earned from the people of the United States, and exercised on behalf of the people of the United States. And the only way we are going to rebuild the American Dream is if we re-take control of our own American government away from these people.

EIRNS/Stuart Lewis

Lyndon LaRouche addresses a Washington, D.C. conference on beam weapon defense April 13, 1983.

Who Is His Opposition?

It is Martin O'Malley's willingness to base his campaign on just such a policy that has gained him the enmity of the establishment media, but even they felt obligated to give prominent coverage, not only to the announcement of his candidacy, but to his forthright attack on Wall Street and insistence on the restoration of Glass-Steagall. *Newsweek*'s headline was: "Attacking Clinton and Wall Street, O'Malley Launches Presidential Bid." Its article noted that it was O'Malley's attacks on Wall Street and Goldman Sachs, and his reference to the "two royal families," that "drew roars from the young, diverse crowd, making it his biggest applause line of the day." Indeed, LaRouchePAC organizers who carried large placards stating GLASS-STEAGALL NOW, were greeted with almost uniform support. A number of those listening to O'Malley, in-

cluding several media and press outlets, sought out LaRouche organizers for a more in-depth explanation of Glass-Steagall.

Not surprisingly, it was the London *Economist* that led the charge against O'Malley. In their May 30 column, "O'Malley flat," they make no mention of his attacks on Wall Street or his call for the restoration of Glass-Steagall (something they clearly see as a *casus belli*), and instead focused on the recent Baltimore riots, saying that they "have unsettled his ambitions, as has Bernie Sanders entering the race." The column goes on to conclude wistfully:

> It is doubtful that Mr. O'Malley will make any dent in Mrs. Clinton's commanding lead.

The same race-baiting line about the Baltimore riots and O'Malley's "Zero Tolerance" police policy, was played widely in other U.S. media, including *Time*, Associated Press, the *Washington Post*, and National Public Radio, both before and after his announcement.

Prior to the Saturday kickoff event, there was constant media hype predicting large protests by a heretofore unheard-of group that claimed that it was O'Malley's policy as Baltimore Mayor that led to the riots. And, their ten to fifteen protesters were given prominent press coverage, despite the fact that none of them were local community activists, or organizers of the protests following the death of Freddie Grey.

What none of that coverage noted, however, was that Martin O'Malley served as Mayor from 1999 to 2007, long before the recent charges levelled at Baltimore's policing policy. They also failed to mention that O'Malley's "Zero Tolerance" policy followed the administration of Kurt Schmoke. It was under Mayor Schmoke that George Soros's drug policies not only dominated City Hall, but turned the city into a virtual free zone for local drug gangs, with one of the highest homicide rates in the nation. O'Malley coupled his crackdown on the drug gangs with "Stop the Killing" marches and vigils through some of the city's worst neighborhoods. Mayor O'Malley's policies enjoyed broad support from community leaders and the black clergy. Several of those leaders were present at the Saturday event to recall that it was in that period, with O'Malley's help, that they successfully took their neighborhoods back from the drug gangs.

Enter Lyndon LaRouche

In recent months, American economist and statesman Lyndon LaRouche has made no secret of the fact that he considers O'Malley to be the only qualified candidate for the Presidency to have emerged so far. In a discussion with supporters May 28 (see "Fireside Chat," this issue), Mr. LaRouche said:

> O'Malley is, on the scale of things, the most prominent figure who might save this nation, as President. Now, that would mean he would have to have not just himself; he would have to have a team. Because a single person as President is not a very effective person. Because the other guys may be going in the other direction.

LaRouche went on to explain:

> So, therefore, the problem is, we have to have, always, we have to have two things: guts, and the teamwork to create a leadership,—a political leadership, a practical leadership,—inside the United States. And we have to pull people together and get them to decide they're going to stick together for that mission.

It is precisely that shaping of the institution of the Presidency that has played a crucial role in LaRouche's work during the entire post-World War II period. LaRouche's key role during the Reagan years, as the intellectual author of Reagan's Strategic Defense Initiative (SDI) policy, has been well documented in this journal. But, the question of just how one shapes the institution of the Presidency is little understood. It doesn't happen as a result of whispering in a President or would-be President's ear. It happens first, instead, in the crafting of a policy that addresses the crucial questions facing the nation at that moment, but then in successfully organizing people,—both those in various positions of leadership and, very importantly, the population at large,—to come together with the needed depth of understanding and passion to fight for that policy.

The Clinton Case

The Clinton Presidency was an instructive case in point. When Clinton ran for his first term as President, Lyndon LaRouche was a political prisoner serving a fifteen-year term in federal prison. Clinton was not viewed with particular favor by those in the LaRouche movement, save for a general agreement that almost anyone was better than Bush, who was instrumental in LaRouche's illegal incarceration. When Clinton actually won the Presidency, LaRouche's supporters continued to bombard Washington, D.C. with demands for LaRouche's exoneration and an end to his incarceration. State legislators and civil rights leaders were joined by delegations of parliamentarians and legal experts from all over the world. Thousands of petition signatures were delivered to the White House. Prominent figures from the United States, and from virtually every continent, lent their names to ads in the *New York Times* and the *Washington Post*.

In 1988, just prior to his incarceration, Lyndon LaRouche had given a press conference at West Berlin's Kempinski Bristol Hotel, on "U.S. Policy Toward the Reunification of Germany." He forecast the collapse of the Comecon economies, and elaborated a "Food for Peace" policy for transforming East-West relations, centered on rebuilding the economy of Poland, so that "the desirable approach to reunification of Germany, can proceed on the basis a majority of Germans on both sides of the Wall desire it should."

A year later, in December 1989, from his prison cell in Rochester, Minnesota, LaRouche commissioned a group of scientists and other specialists from the Schiller Institute to work out an economic program for Europe, known as the "Productive Triangle." In January 1990, "The Productive Triangle, Paris-Berlin-Vienna: Locomotive for the World Economy," was published in German. This geographical area, a spherical triangle approximately as large as the territory of Japan, encompassing the industrial regions of northern France, western and eastern Germany, and parts of former Czechoslovakia and Austria, was envisioned to serve as a locomotive to restart the collapsing world economy.

The "Triangle" program aimed at stimulating the economy of eastern and western Europe following the fall of the "Iron Curtain," by means of large projects for the modernization of infrastructure in transportation, energy, water, and communications. These projects, to be financed chiefly through state credit at low rates of interest, would stimulate the demand for investment goods over the long term, secure employment, and favor the creation of modern industrial factories. The

Chris Desley

A LaRouche movement rally in defense of the Clinton Presidency in Sacramento, Calif. on Jan. 7, 1999.

backbone of the triangle was to be an integrated system of high-speed and magnetic levitation rail, to be used for transport of both passengers and freight. The transportation network was to be expanded with roads and waterways, linked by automated freight-transfer systems. The urban centers would be connected with magnetic levitation lines.

During the five years of LaRouche's incarceration, his wife, Helga Zepp-LaRouche travelled the world building a vast network of support, including in Russia and the nations that had previously comprised the Soviet Union.

When LaRouche's supporters in the United States finally made successful contact with Clinton Administration officials in the effort to win his release from prison, it turned out that what had captured the attention of the new President, more than any other single factor, was that policy. It was the beginning of an infor-

mal collaboration that ultimately led to Clinton's insistence on the need for a "New Financial Architecture," a policy that mirrored LaRouche's decades-long fight for a New Bretton Woods. It also made Clinton a target of the London/Wall Street-centered financial oligarchy that ultimately orchestrated his impeachment. Although they succeeded in formal impeachment proceedings, Clinton managed to hold on to the Presidency.

When, in 1998, it was learned that Joe Lieberman, then a Democratic Senator from Connecticut and later Al Gore's Vice Presidential nominee, was organizing a Democratic Congressional group to visit Clinton and demand his resignation, the LaRouche movement launched the "Committee to Save the Presidency," pulling together a broad coalition of state legislators from across the U.S., and exposing who and what was really behind the London-based war on the very institution of the Presidency. Later, close Clinton associates gratefully acknowledged that it was largely that effort that saved Clinton's Presidency. But, unfortunately, the institution itself, which was already infected with the likes of Al Gore, who was consistently working against the embattled President, had been seriously weakened. It was during this period that a badly distracted Clinton signed the repeal of Glass-Steagall, something he today acknowledges was a grave error.

Later, during both John Kerry's 2004 Presidential campaign and then Hillary Clinton's 2008 campaign, the informal collaboration continued, and indeed intensified. Most of the specific details of that collaboration are subject to agreements of confidentiality, but they are nevertheless obvious in terms of policy direction, both domestically and internationally.

Coming back to the present situation, there is no question that so far, O'Malley has exhibited both the courage and the understanding to qualify for the Presidency. But there is much work that has to be done, not only in pulling together the components of a team for governance after the 2016 election, but for what must essentially serve as a transitional Presidency right now, taking power away from Barack Obama, whose current policies could very well lead us to nuclear war.

Will Europe Survive The Collapse of the Euro System?

by Helga Zepp-LaRouche

June 2—While the Greek crisis is coming to a head, maybe this week, but certainly in the remaining weeks of June, the idea of a unified European Union (EU) has become as full of holes as the proverbial swiss cheese. As this article is being published, ultimatums are flying.

No matter whether Greece suspends payment on the 300 million euros it owes the IMF this Friday, June 5, because it cannot accept further austerity measures demanded by the Troika, such as raising taxes in the range of 3.5 billion euros and further cuts in social services; or whether the European Central Bank, German Chancellor Angela Merkel and French President François Hollande at the last moment propose a somewhat less brutal austerity program; either way, within the current EU logic there is no way out, either for Greece, or for the EU.

Because after June 5, further payments by Greece come due: on June 12, 350 million euros; on June 16, 600 million; on June 19, 345 million; and then, altogether Greece has a debt of 350 billion (!). If the proverbial miracle does not occur, such as the creditors agreeing to the European debt conference demanded by Greece—the chances of which are currently totally impossible—the policy of the EU will drive Greece into insolvency. At that point, and not at the end of the 30-day grace period, which theoretically exists before Greece technically enters definite insolvency, there is a threat of a general collapse of the European banks, and, as a result of the derivatives exposure and swap-arrangements between the ECB and the Fed, a collapse of the American financial sector as well.

The faction of those who swear that a "Grexit" would be bearable, even somewhat "prediscounted," such as IMF head Christine Lagarde and occasionally German Finance Minister Wolfgang Schäuble, insists at the same time on compliance with the draconian austerity pact, because they fear that a concession by the Troika would have a signal effect on the other countries which have been forced to their knees by brutal austerity pacts, such as Spain, Portugal, Italy, and even France. Behind this view lies the calculation that it would be better for Greece, having returned to the drachma and having been reduced to beggary, to serve as a horrifying example for the other potential candidates for leaving the euro, rather than to accept a weakening of fiscal discipline, and with it, the end of the euro.

Panicked warnings have come especially from the United States, such as the one from U.S. Treasury Sec-

The Kremlin

Greek Prime Minister Alexis Tsipras meets Russian President Putin in the Kremlin April 8, in the midst of Greece's showdown with the European Union.

retary Jack Lew, that a Grexit would have dramatic consequences for the world financial system. Paul Krugman warned in a June 1 article in the *New York Times* with the headline "That 1914 Feeling," that the inability of the Europeans to solve the Greek crisis is an eerie reminder of the miscalculations leading to the First World War—Krugman quoted, as he said, the latest book by Christopher Clark about the background of the First World War, *The Sleepwalkers.* Krugman then compares the errors of judgment, even the enthusiasm, with which the Europeans leapt over the cliff in 1914, with the nonchalance today about Greece. Does Krugman, in using this ominous metaphor, know more than he dares to write?

Eurozone Fracturing

Italian Finance Minister Pier Carlo Padoan reflected another variant on Fantasy-Island thinking, when he went so far as to rave that after a Grexit, the Euro-Zone will be a totally different entity (namely one from which countries can simply walk out), but that such a Grexit would be a welcome development which would expedite the further integration of Europe.

Apparently Mr. Padoan doesn't often read newspapers. British Prime Minister David Cameron made an appearance with Hollande and Merkel, that Great Britain's membership in the EU could only survive Britain's upcoming referendum if the EU Treaty were changed, and gave back more autonomy to the states. And Mrs. Merkel, in apparent affinity with Cameron and realizing that the EU would not survive a "Brexit," even promised to be open to renegotiating the EU Treaty. The notion that, under current circumstances, the twenty-eight EU member states could agree on a new EU Treaty, suffers from a horribly far-reaching lack of reality.

Not only was the Lisbon Treaty of 2007 only adopted through conspiratorial maneuvers—everything was decided on the level of the European Council behind closed doors, and the members of the Euro parliament from the different nations were given a modified text of the constitution that was rejected in 2005 in France and Holland, which had been turned into a mere treaty that was not subject to a referendum,—but in such an incomprehensible form that almost nobody read it. Ever since, the EU has been hated for its lack of transparency, its arrogance, and its policies favoring the bankers at the expense of the general welfare,—by the greater part of the population, and this is not only in the southern European states.

The much-vaunted unity of Europe has the consistency of Swiss cheese. The EU bureaucrats and technocrats want a United States of Europe as quickly as possible. Great Britain wants more autonomy, because otherwise Scotland's independence, and not only that, would turn it into Little Britain. Great Britain, Scandinavia, and the Baltic states have degenerated into truly hysterical warmongering against Russia, while the Czech Republic, Slovakia, Hungary, and Greece openly demand an end to the sanctions against Russia.

Two former German Chancellors, Helmut Schmidt and Gerhard Schröder, are extremely critical of Merkel, because she has, for the second time, disinvited Russian President Putin from the Group of Seven Summit; so are Eckard Cordes, the chairman of the Committee on Eastern European Economic Relations, as well as the German Association of Machine-Builders (the VDMA), and the German Mittelstand. The fact that German machinery exports to Russia collapsed in the first quarter by around 28%, while U.S. exports to Russia increased around 17%, strengthens the suspicion many Germans have that the sanctions forced through by the United States and Great Britain not only have the goal of regime change in Russia, but that the old Anglo-American geopolitical impulse has also been directed against Germany.

People in America don't have the slightest inkling of how the NSA affair, in all its aspects—from the tapping of Mrs. Merkel's cell phone, to industrial espionage and the total spying on the population—has eroded the German-American relationship. The fact that the NSA and BND (the German Federal Intelligence Service) together have monitored and spied not only on private industry, but also on politicians in France, Austria and Belgium, is a fission fungus in Europe. Merkel's famous statement—"Spying among friends does not function at all"—has become a synonym for the realization that this is obviously not a matter among friends, but the pursuit of war against a specific population.

If you soberly consider the real situation in the EU today, you can only conclude that the euro was clearly, from the beginning, a failed experiment: Not only that the Eurozone was never an ideal currency sphere,—it was totally obvious that a currency union between

The BRICS alternative to the EU is presented in this election campaign poster of Tom Gillesburg, running for the Danish Parliament.

states as different as highly industrialized Germany, and agrarian states such as Greece or Portugal couldn't last. But the evil intention from the side of Margaret Thatcher, François Mitterrand, and George Bush Sr. in 1989, to impose the euro on Germany for geopolitical reasons, as the price for German reunification, was to take revenge. At least in the case of Mitterrand, an adviser and eminence grise of the Socialist Party, Jacques Attali, reported that Mitterrand threatened former German Chancellor Kohl with war, if Kohl were not ready to give up the Deutschemark. All three—Thatcher, Mitterrand, and Bush—were agreed that Germany must be checked, and wedged into the straitjacket of the Maastricht Treaty, in order to weaken its economy and thus to prevent it from building up an independent economic relationship with Russia,—something which was always a thorn in the eye of the Imperial powers, especially since the Rapallo Treaty of 1923,—and against which they would even resort to political assassination.

It is remarkable that Helmut Schmidt has recently identified the trigger for the Ukraine crisis, which he sees now threatening to develop into a "hot war," as the Maastricht Treaty, through which the foundation for the expansion of the EU toward the East was laid, without regard for Russia and history. "EU membership was offered to countries like Ukraine or remote Georgia, to turn them in the direction of the West." Former French President Valerie Giscard D'Estaing, a political contemporary of Schmidt, attested several days ago to many historical facts showing that Crimea has never belonged to Ukraine.

Will There Be a Break?

The disillusionment, if not the frustration, of the citizens of various European nations with the EU has reached seismic proportions. Far from strengthening and uniting Europe, the discord among nations is greater than at any time since the Second World War. The initial feeling of a "democracy deficit" has expanded into the widely prevalent feeling that democracy in Europe is dead. (Indicative of the mood in Germany is the latest satire of "The Institution" of May 26.

Among an ever-larger part of the European population, frustration over the mediocre quality of the politicians has solidified. The Euro-skeptic parties are winning in droves, as shown in the recent elections in Spain, Italy, Austria, and Great Britain. Whether it's Merkel with her policy of little steps, or Hollande, with his catastrophic poll ratings—these so-called leading personalities are seen at best as crisis-managers, who are panting behind events without developing the slightest vision for the future, or presenting serious solutions to the multiplying crises.

For this reason, as well as the growing fear of a great war, which threatens to develop out of the provocations by NATO and the U.S. against Russia and China—the policy of the New Silk Road of China, and especially the offer of Chinese President Xi Jinping for an inclusive "Win-Win Policy," is gaining ever greater attraction. If Churchill's dictum were true, that in politics there are no friends—which is obviously confirmed by the NSA—but only interests, then the interests of Europe are better served by working together with the nations of the BRICS.

A Rail Revolution for the U.S. Economy

by Jeffrey Steinberg

June 1—In his weekly dialogue with the LaRouchePAC Policy Committee May 25, Lyndon LaRouche spelled out the urgent need for the United States to launch a nationwide high-speed rail system, as a means of transforming the U.S. economy and reconstituting a qualified 21st-Century labor force, in the aftermath of two generations of economic collapse and near-total loss of the productive power of labor.

LaRouche invoked the revolution in labor power that was initiated by President Abraham Lincoln, through his promotion of the Transcontinental Railroad, even as the British prepared their Confederate secessionist drive to destroy the Union.

LaRouche's remarks provide a perfect framework for looking back on Lincoln's vision of an invincible continental republic, which was at the heart of his lifetime commitment to the Transcontinental Railroad, and to the advancement of American labor power.

The Rail System Is the Secret

LaRouche told the May 25 session:

The only way that you can [revive the real economy of the United States], is by creating a transportation system which is based on the railroad concept. (**Figure 1**) You've got to think about,

FIGURE 1

The Proposed 42,000-Mile-Long Network of National Electrified Rail

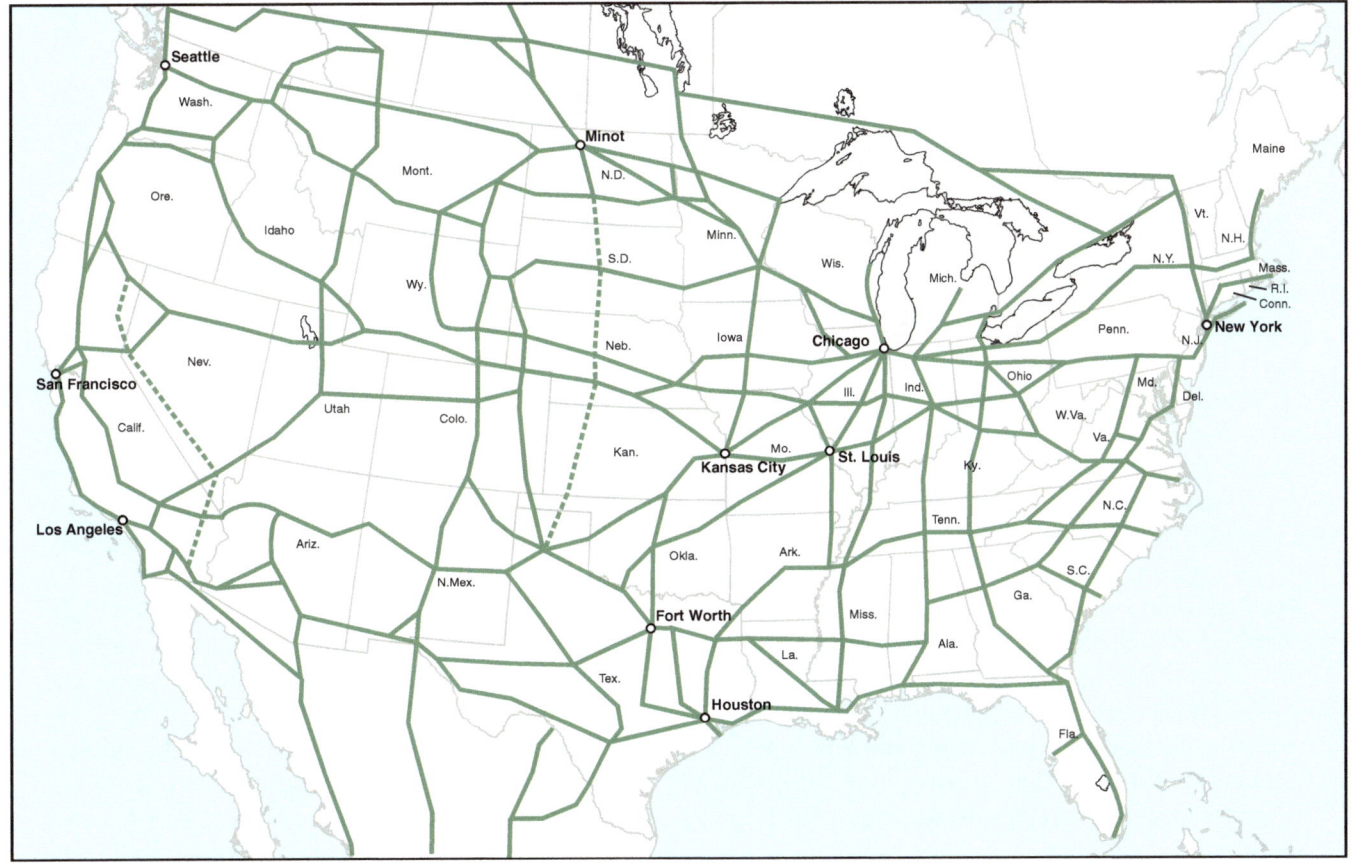

EIRNS/Alan Yue

A 2005 plan for a 42,000-mile U.S. high-speed, electrified rail system, designed by transportation consultant Hal S. Cooper. The directions of connection, by Alaska Railroad to the Bering Strait and Eurasia, and to Central and South America, are obvious.

how can you produce a productivity factor, among the ranks of the people of the United States? What industry, what particular thing that is feasible?

Now, what China has been doing with rails, for example, is a signal to the United States as to what the United States has to do to recover the economy of the United States.

I mean, you can't say, 'we're going to get you money for this, money for this, money for that'—that doesn't work. Handouts don't work! What you've got to do is, you've got to take a part of the labor force which is not yet capable of doing the job. But you build that labor force, you bring them into function around a cadre group, but it has to be one thing: Transportation. Mass transportation, freight and people. And whereas you start that process, it means that everything that you're doing in terms of innovation, is now going to be a contribution to the economy and the development of the economy of the United States, *and* of the labor force, the productivity of the labor force. And that's what we have to do.

So you start with the Manhattan idea, but you say this is only the core of the thing. Then you go with the rest of the project, and you build an effect. And we're going to get echoes, from South America, Peru, etc., etc. It's already coming. So we will have that. Then we can be allied with forces such as India, Russia, China, and so forth. That's all there.

And we're going to have to have big fights, because the threats in these various parts of the planet are very serious; mass killing, mass death, that's the program. But we have to have a mechanism, which in itself generates growth of the economy of the United States and other nations. Then we use that, in the way where it's supplied, but check on the case where you can get the best and quickest effort; and the building of a high-speed, multiple-function, railroad system, of a modern type, a really modern type. And you build up a whole territory, so that you begin to integrate the areas of the United States. Only rails can do that.

So you have a railroad system, use that as a training system for people.

The Lincoln Revolution

But it's the transportation system, the train system, which is the most efficient, quickest way, to develop the economy, which we did already before, in the 19th Century. We already did that! The rail system is the secret of how you can build the economy of the United States, and rebuild it. It's a new kind of rail system, but the principle is still the same: You're taking people, almost as novices; you're training them, you're putting them to work while you're training them, and you're developing skills among them, by training....

You've got to think about what the condition of the employable population in the United States is today, the potentially employable; and realize that they don't have any skills as such. And what kind of jobs are you going to give them, what kind of development are you going to give them? Well, they don't have a practical job which is a self-paying job. In other words, you get people, you start to train them, you build the process up. You're now doing something, you're increasing the productivity of the national economy. It starts a little slower, at first, but it becomes very rapid, because the technology is well-known. And you've got technology, you've got business that will go to China and so forth, where the railroad system is going on; what's going on in India, and so forth—of nations which are actually involved in building high-speed-rail systems, which are needed.

And you move as fast as you can. So you're not doing something, like bit, bit, bit-by-bit nonsense. You're going in with a clean sweep, to turn brilliance into being. And that's what you do.

It was done before, by us, as in the Civil War period under Lincoln, where it became really—that became the driver which continued to determine the United States, into, actually, the 20th Century. And that's what we need to do. But we need to have a sense of organization, of how we structure the creation of the organization needed to make this effect, and make it very quickly efficient, for the average citizen of the United States.

The best starting point for creating what LaRouche has called for is to revisit the Lincoln revolution.

Lincoln's Land-Bridge: The Transcontinental Campaign

The following is excerpted from a presentation by Jeffrey Steinberg on Feb. 1, 2003, titled, "Lincoln's Railroad and the European Land-Bridge Today," and published in EIR, March 28, 2003.

Abraham Lincoln was born in 1809. He was 20 years old when the first successful test of a locomotive on a railroad was accomplished, in England. And within a few short years of that, by 1832, at the age of 22-23, Lincoln was running for the state legislature in Illinois, on a platform of building a transcontinental railroad.

Lincoln understood that to defeat the power of oligarchism—particularly the British, with their various French and Hapsburg allies—required that the entire American continental republic had to be consolidated. When he campaigned for the state legislature on this idea of a transcontinental railroad, Lincoln had never seen a railroad, never ridden on one. There were a few beginning to be constructed on the East Coast of the United States. But nothing as far out into the western part of the colonized United States as Illinois. Talk about not being stuck in sense-certainty.

Nevertheless, he understood a concept that provided an absolutely unique solution to a grave crisis, which was that the Union was in jeopardy.

After the John Quincy Adams Presidency, 1824-28, we had a real string of losers, starting with Andrew Jackson, then Martin Van Buren, and then, Buchanan and Polk; and really, the condition of the political parties in the United States, by the time that the Republican Party was founded in the early 1850s, was as bad, maybe even worse than the situation right now: total corruption, complete irrelevance. And so Lincoln was the great man of vision of this period. And he understood that the railroad issue was absolutely fundamental to everything.

FIGURE 2
America's Transcontinental Railroads, as Built from the Eastern Rail System After 1865

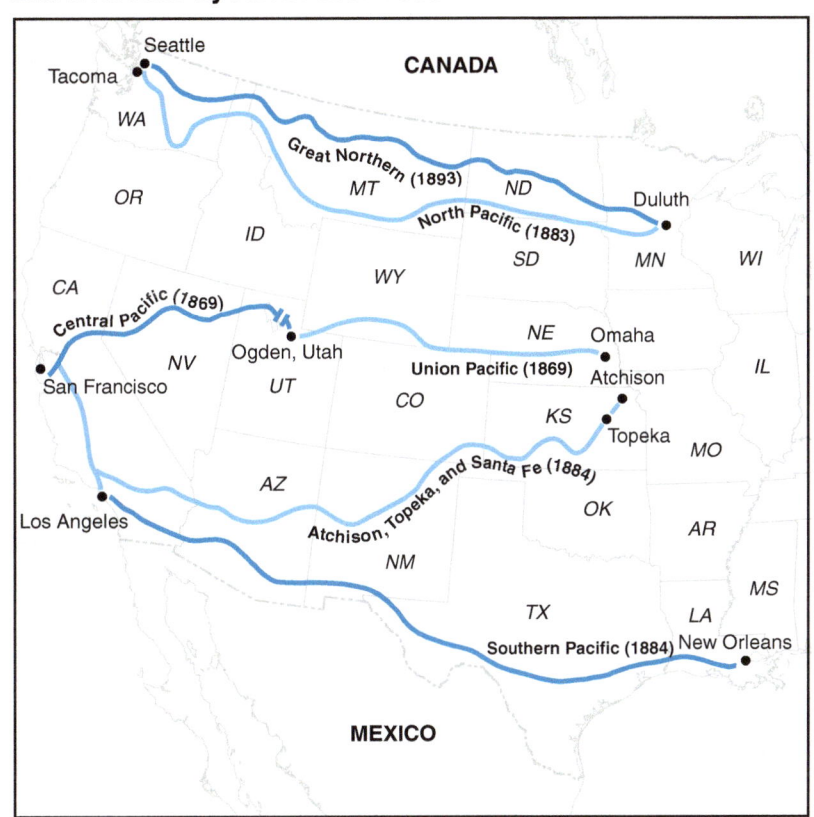

Source: EIR

In 1862, Lincoln signed the Pacific Railway Act to create a Transcontinental Railroad, with a direct government role through surveying, land grants, and government bond financing. By 1893, a total of five transcontinental railroads were constructed.

Four years later, he was elected to the Illinois legislature, and again, made the issue of railroads a major focus. In fact, what he proposed was a Federal law that would grant Federally owned land to the states, so that the states could sell the land, or use it otherwise, to begin launching major railroad projects. He proposed the creation of quasi-public corporations to build these railroads. And it's a measure of the success of Lincoln's policy—along with many other people—that by 1856, the Illinois Central Railroad was the largest railroad in the world, and one of the largest corporations. And Lincoln made sure that there were regulations and other legislation that made this all possible. This was one of the important test cases of the American System of political economy.

By 1853, this railroad issue had reached the point that, by Act of Congress, a survey was commissioned to figure out the best route for a transcontinental railroad. At the time that this was happening (**Figure 2**), Omaha,

Neb. was the farthest-west point of development of the United States. Nebraska was not even a state at that time. But Omaha was on one side of the Missouri River; Cedar Bluff, Iowa was on the other side; and that was it. The next U.S. city, the only city between Omaha and Sacramento, Calif., was Salt Lake City. The rest of the western portion of the United States, out to the Pacific Coast, was underdeveloped, untapped. You had had, in 1804-6, the Lewis and Clark expedition, which went out and started looking into these areas of the country. But there was nothing out there.

A Continental Republic

So here you are talking about a transcontinental railroad, which first and foremost, involves undertaking a massive survey of, approximately, the western two-thirds of the United States. Because ultimately, the distance from the beginning to the end of the Transcontinental Railroad would be a little over 2,000 miles. You had a massive survey operation that was conducted over a period of years, in which, for the first time, that whole western part of the United States was mapped out and visited. These were areas which hadn't even really been broken through with very many trails.

When you had the discovery of gold in California in the late 1840s, and the Gold Rush commenced, generally speaking, to get from the East Coast to California, you had three alternative routes that you could take. You could go overland, which was a pretty daunting task; you had about a 50% survival rate if you were really in good health, 18-25 years old, and it took six months. You could take a train, by that point, somewhat into the Midwest. But from there on, it was a long walk; or with carriages and horses; it wasn't a very easy route.

You had a second option, which was to go by boat to Panama; and there was no Panama Canal then, but the Isthmus was pretty narrow; and if you could avoid dying of malaria or smallpox, or other diseases, and you could get out to the Pacific Coast of Panama, and then be lucky enough not to have to wait for months to catch a boat, you could catch a boat on from there up to San Francisco. And that also took—if you were lucky, and made a very good connection between the boats—about six months.

The third, safest option, was to go by boat from ports on the East Coast, all the way around Cape Horn.

If you were lucky—and if you could afford it—that usually took between 200 and 220 days. And again, the prospects of making it in one piece were not all that great.

In other words, the idea that we had a continental republic that was a single, unified political entity, was just not true. Yet Lincoln, and Henry Clay, and Henry Carey and the other key Whig figures, republicans, understood that without that continental republic being consolidated, the United States was finished. And this whole experiment in republican government, which was a global mission, would not survive.

Here you've got a situation where the United States is targeted for destruction by the British. This is not something that began the day that Lincoln was elected. It had been building up for a very long time.

So one of the things that happened when this massive land survey occurred—and it was done under the War Department; the Secretary of War at the time was a guy named Jefferson Davis, who would later become the President of the Confederacy, so you get an idea that there were some political complications here— various routes came back; and Davis recommended that the route that should be chosen, ran through the Southern states. It should run from the Louisiana Purchase, through Texas, through the New Mexico and Arizona areas, and out to California through that route. There was no way that the republican faction, the American System faction, was going to let that happen.

So the issue was under consideration, but was dead because of the politics in Washington, until Lincoln was elected. But there was a paradox. Because within days after Lincoln's election, the Southern War of Secession started. You have to really take in the situation that Lincoln took in, because Lincoln was, remember, for 30 years, convinced that the survival of the United States was tied to the Transcontinental Railroad project. And he understood that this was not merely an American project; this was a model for use in many other parts of the world. And we were already actively helping to build up plans and actually build up the rail infrastructure in Russia at the same time.

'It's the 42nd Parallel'

There was a famous incident in Lincoln's life, where, in 1859, he was visiting Cedar Bluff, Iowa—in fact, he was giving a campaign speech. He was introduced by a mutual friend, to a man named Grenville Dodge, who was the number-one railroad builder in the United States; he was an engineer. Dodge had been directly involved in some of the survey projects into the Western states. In fact, Dodge's teacher, his engineering instructor, had just come back from doing major exploration out in the Puget Sound area, and had just completed a six-month journey, mapping out the land routes potentially usable for the Transcontinental Railroad.

So Lincoln, in 1859, in this chance encounter with Dodge, sat down with him; and he asked him one question: What's the best route out to the Pacific Coast for the railroad? And Dodge had the maps right there in hand, and he said, "It's the 42nd Parallel."

This was all going on as the war clouds were gathering over the United States. Dodge went to Chicago, to the Republican Party nominating convention, and was one of Lincoln's delegates. Shortly after that, he went to Washington to meet with Lincoln, who, even though he understood that war was about to break out, knew that the United States had to launch the Transcontinental Railroad project *at that very moment*.

There were a lot of things involved in this. There was the fundamental issue in Lincoln's mind—and Lyn has discussed this concept over and over again—that the key to warfare is winning the peace. If you have to go to war, you've already failed in the mission of keeping the peace; but if you have to go to war, from the very outset, you have to define war-winning objectives, objectives that will enable you to win the war and secure a better condition of life for both the victors and the vanquished; so that you actually succeed in laying the foundations for a durable peace. And for Lincoln, the issue was the Transcontinental

Union Gen. Grenville Dodge epitomized the Civil War veteran officers whose military experience made the Transcontinental Railroad possible: he was the nation's pre-eminent railroad engineer, and the real progress of the railroad's construction had to await his relief from active duty after the War's end.

Railroad.

He had some friends and allies in this. And this process, as exciting as it was, was very messy. The American people, during this period, were not exclusively saints. There were people who profiteered. There were people who did all sorts of things that, in some cases, landed them in jail. But it's how real economics works. These things are not neat and clean. They're not theoretical. Above all else, the key question is leadership. Because under the right leadership, you can force people, even against their worst intentions, to contribute to the good. And you will see that that was the organizing principle that Lincoln used in the Transcontinental Railroad project.

You had a bunch of people who had gone out to California in the Gold Rush of 1849; it was actually their accounts of their travels, which gave this picture of what it was like, going from New York or Boston to San Francisco in the period before the Transcontinental Railroad was completed. It was absolutely hell. So you had this bunch of people who became leading investors in the railroad. But the most important of those who went out to California, was [at the time, Lieutenant] William Tecumseh Sherman. He had just graduated from West Point, class of 1840, and was sent out to California during the Mexican War on a military assignment. After the Mexican War, he left the military and became a prominent banker and leading political figure in San Francisco; and also became one of the most important boosters of the Transcontinental Railroad.

To give an idea of what the demographics of California looked like at this time: 1850 is when California reached a large enough population to win statehood. At that point, there were 94,000 people living in the state, of whom only 7,000 were female. By 1860, the popula-

Gen. William Tecumseh Sherman, as a businessman in California after the Civil War, became both an investor in, and leading organizer of the completion of the Transcontinental. Another Lincoln Republican, Leland Stanford, led the railroad construction east from Sacramento. Here, the "Jupiter" carries Stanford to the Golden Spike ceremony in Utah.

tion was 433,000. So you get an idea of the phenomenal population growth, even before the railroad was completed. And by the way, by 1860, the population of California included 53,000 Chinese, who came over here, not as slave labor, but because the opportunity to get decent wages were greater than anything available in China. There were a lot of problems; there was racism; there were all sorts of terrible things done; but this was basically not a new kind of slavery. And you'll see that the Chinese played an absolutely indispensable role in the Transcontinental Railroad.

Railroad To Win the Peace

The fight for the railroad coincided with the outbreak of the Civil War. But nevertheless, Lincoln was absolutely committed to the idea of launching this project even as the war was going on; and in some cases, even in the very darkest days of the Civil War.

By May 6, 1862, the House of Representatives passed the Pacific Railroad Bill; and about a month and a half later, on June 20, it was passed by the Senate. Because of the demands of the war, the idea of the railroad being built as a government project, per se, was out of the question. Nevertheless, it gives you an idea of the different means by which the government could play an absolutely pivotal role in directing this kind of great national project.

Under the original 1862 law, provision was made for creating two quasi-public corporations. One, was the Central Pacific Railroad; and the other was the Union Pacific Railroad. The Central Pacific was already in the works. And among the people who were involved in it were William T. Sherman and Leland Stanford, who was a Lincoln Republican, and became governor of California in 1860. They were among the wealthiest people in the state, and were among the investors in the original Central Pacific Railroad project.

The Union Pacific was set up by a group of people back East; but the provision was that these two rail lines would be built with the Central Pacific starting out in Sacramento, and moving eastward; and the Union Pacific starting out in Omaha and going westward. The idea was that they would meet up at some point in between, and Congress was very careful not to predetermine where that point would be.

There were a lot of things that went into this project, particularly at the point the War ended. But the point is, that this thing started while the Civil War was going on. This was something quite extraordinary: that Lincoln had this vision of what it would take to win the peace;

and he knew that there could be no compromise, no armistice, that the Confederacy, this British insurrection, had to be absolutely defeated; but that at the same time, there had to be a great national mission and project that would define the war-winning objective, and would be an instrumentality for healing the terrible wounds of the Civil War.

You'll see that that's precisely what happened, even though most of the work was done after Lincoln was assassinated.

The project was launched. The Union Pacific recognized that to do this thing right, the person that they had to have in charge as the chief engineer, was Grenville Dodge. Except,

Chinese immigrants played an important role in building the Central Pacific through the Sierra Nevada Mountains, using experience from road-building along river cliffs in China.

by this point, Dodge was a general in the Union Army, and there was no way he was going to resign his commission to go to work building a railroad, until the insurrection had been defeated. In fact, he was one of the most important figures in the Union Army. He was the general serving immediately under William T. Sherman, heading up the engineering division, and played a critical role in the flanking maneuver that ultimately led to the march and sacking of Atlanta, a critical turning point in the Civil War. What Dodge did during the War was real on-the-job training for what was done with the Transcontinental Railroad, because his main mission was building rail lines, repairing lines that had been sabotaged by fleeing Confederate forces, and building bridges over rivers that had been destroyed, again, by retreating Confederate forces.

So one obstacle was that the person singularly most qualified to do the job was occupied—justifiably so, but occupied—until the Spring of 1866.

The Physical Obstacles

There were a lot of challenges. I don't know how many of you have had a chance to explore around the Sierra Nevada Mountains, with their enormous walls of granite. To actually create a rail line linking Sacramento

and San Francisco, you had to figure out some way to get through the Sierra Nevadas. And at this point, the technology available was extremely primitive. This was one of the ways that the Chinese played a very extraordinary role.

The first phase of the construction work was the surveying of land that had really never been surveyed before. The question was, how are we going to build rail lines through granite mountains? What are we going to do about the bridging technology to get very heavy track and very heavy trains going over river beds, through these mountain gorges, which in some cases were very high up and spanned fairly substantial distances? The person who had invented the bridge-and-trestle system was Leonardo da Vinci. And the next major technological advances were made on the construction of the Transcontinental Railroad.

The Chinese were instrumental, because in China, over many centuries, there had been experience with, for example, building roadbeds along the Yangtze River, with mountainous cliffs on the side. To give you an idea of how they did this: The crews that had to cut through major tunnels in the Sierra Nevadas—once they had even figured out where to do it with the most efficient routes—you had these crews starting on both

Just west of the juncture at Promontory Point, Utah, a 2,000-man Central Pacific crew laid an unprecedented 10 miles of track in one day. Shown: Central Pacific crews at Camp Victory, west of Promontory Summit, Utah (photo by Alfred A. Hart, 1869).

ended in 1865, this project became the number-one nation-building, nation-healing, high-paying job for the tens of thousands of Civil War veterans—generally 18-20-year-old kids who had fought on either the Union or the Confederate side—this project defined a national mission that helped reunify the country after the Civil War, and after all of the scars of the War. It was a national project that everyone took pride in, and it was an opportunity for people who would have been in much worse shape if you didn't have this kind of major jobs program going on.

This was the project under which many, many Chinese people came to the United States, and immediately had access to some of the highest-

sides of the mountain. One question—not an inconsequential engineering issue—was whether or not the two sides were going eventually to converge, or waste a lot of time and miss the route. These were—not necessarily Brunelleschi's Dome—but these were very serious engineering challenges.

The way it actually worked, was that at the peak of building of these tunnels, they would have three crews working 24 hours a day, 8-hour shifts; Chinese workers, basically with hammers and drill bits, would hammer holes into the granite, and initially, they would basically stuff the hole with black powder explosives. They'd light the fuses, step back; then they'd have to lug away whatever rock was blown. And on the average, on a good day, taking the whole face of the tunnel, they'd get somewhere between 6 and 12 inches a day. So you're talking about colossal engineering tasks here. And it took quite a number of months to do. Eventually, this became the first project where dynamite black powder was replaced by the use of nitroglycerin, which significantly sped up, in the latter phases of the project, the tunneling aspects.

These were engineering feats that had never been achieved before. From the point that the Civil War

paying jobs in the country. And they did an absolutely extraordinary job, principally working on the Central Pacific line coming east from California. Most of the workers on the westbound line were Civil War veterans, some from the South, a lot from the North; a lot of Irish. And at the peak point, on any given day there were 30,000 people working full-time on the construction of the railroad. It was done, eventually, after Dodge retired from the Union Army. And his last assignment was under Sherman in the Western territories of Mississippi and Missouri, where they also had to do a lot of negotiating with the Indians, in order to secure these projects as they were going forward. Very tricky, very messy.

Financing and City-Building

The way that the Federal government funded the railroad project, as a national project, was that the two corporations—the Central Pacific and the Union Pacific—were pledged a certain amount of money in low-interest Federal bonds for every mile of track that they completed, and which was certified as having been constructed up to par, by government inspectors. And they received, usually, $12,000 per mile for flat track,

$36,000 per mile for graded track, and $48,000 per mile for these specially challenging areas, up through the mountains, and things like that. They were also given land grants. The Federal government owned most of the land in the area. So the railroad companies were given land grants for the land adjacent to the rail line.

But the most important thing, is that—imagine the situation, say, for the Union Pacific line going westbound from Omaha. There's nothing ahead of you until you hit the Salt Lake in Utah; and it was at the Salt Lake where the two lines actually met and the Golden Spike was laid.

So, really, you're going through an area where there is not so much as a village along the way. So, in a sense, you're using the same kind of military logistics that you would use to move an army forward. Because you're bringing all of your supplies behind you, and as you're moving the track forward, you're bringing all of that along. And at certain critical points, they designated areas where they would build cities, because they needed to be building more rolling stock, railroad cars, locomotives. So, in other words, the major cities along the route of the Transcontinental Railroad were built as part of the project itself.

It was even more difficult from the standpoint of the Central Pacific, because everything that they got had to come by boat, either around Cape Horn, or through the Panama Isthmus, so they had even more daunting costs and logistical challenges. Everything had to go to the West Coast, and then come back East.

At a certain point, in the Winter of 1866-67, and again in 1867-68, that whole area of the country experienced the worst blizzards in recorded memory. And so, the decision was made by the Central Pacific, that the only way that they could move along fast on schedule, was by actually building sheds over the track. So that as they moved the track forward, they were actually building these wooden sheds, so that if there were avalanches of snow, they went off on the side, and they didn't destroy the track. What they built, as simply a temporary part of the construction logistics, was what was called the "biggest house in the world." One segment alone, was a single uninterrupted wooden structure that ran 29 miles long.

So there was a lot of innovation on this project as well. And there were also a lot of problems.

One problem originated the term "hell on wheels,"

because what happened is, that since this was the largest construction project, certainly in the history of North America, with tens of thousands of workers getting paid cash on the job, wherever the railroad was, there were these roving whorehouses, saloons, tents that would pop up overnight, gambling dens, prostitution houses; and so you had a whole sort of criminal apparatus that was parasitizing off this project. You know, you had young guys—as I said, in 1850, there were only 7,000 women in the entire state of California. I can assure you, there were none along the construction route, other than these mobile crews, this "hell on wheels."

So, as I say, it was an imperfect phenomenon. Real people were doing it. But because there was a top-down sense of a national mission, and a certain commitment that the future of the country was at stake, and that there was a great precedent being set, even with all of these problems, things got done in a miraculous way.

You also had Wall Street swindlers, who made a killing on this. In fact, shortly after the completion of the Transcontinental Railroad, a number of the top executives of the Union Pacific went to jail. One of my favorites was a guy named Francis Train, who was a relative of John Train—one of the nasty Wall Street characters involved in the "railroad" trial of Lyndon LaRouche. Very important guy. But it was his family that set up a construction company called Crédit Mobilier of America, and they were convinced there was no money to be made in the railroads. They were convinced that the money to be made, was through skimming off of the government guarantees of bonds to cover the construction costs. So, some of the top executives of the Union Pacific set up, with Train, Crédit Mobilier, as a construction company that they hired to do all of the work on the project. And so there were points toward the end, where the workers were not getting their wages, but where the investors in Crédit Mobilier were getting 300% of their investments back in dividend payment. So this is the kind of thing you were dealing with.

There were government regulations, there were all sorts of provisions for the government money in the form of land grants and bonds, but it was done with a lot of imperfection. The kind of thing that you wouldn't allow to happen the next time around; but again, the point is that all of this was still, nevertheless, vectored into this great project.

Library of Congress

The telegraph which was strung across the United States with the Transcontinental Railroad, continued, with Russian collaboration, all the way to St. Petersburg.

An International Project Mission

Another aspect of the Transcontinental Railroad project was that, all along the way, attached to the rail crews, were the telegraph crews. So that for the first time in the United States history, and the first time probably in history of anywhere, telegraph lines were being built that would eventually connect the entire United States. And as part of the understandings that Lincoln had worked out with the Russians, the telegraph lines actually went uninterruptedly, by the end of the Civil War, from Washington, D.C. to St. Petersburg, Russia. In other words, there were crews in Russia that were building the lines from San Francisco up the coast, over the Bering Strait, down to Vladivostok, and on to St. Petersburg, so that there was a U.S.-Russian integrated telegraph system. That also tells you very clearly, that the rail project was something that was not an American-only project; it was something that was intended to be part of a global revolution, that the American System republicans were carrying out.

We finally reach the point, in May of 1869, that the rail line was finished. And I think the final anecdote on the construction is sort of interesting,

By this time, you had, really, an incredible engineering capability that had been developed, through the course of this seemingly impossible project. And in fact, much of the rapid development, the city-building, and massive expanded railroad construction that occurred after this, was done by the people who built the Transcontinental Railroad. They developed extraordinary engineering skills. Dodge, who lived until 1916, continued for the rest of his life—he never retired; he continued right up until his death building railroads, the last one being in Cuba.

But these crews became so proficient, that a week before the Golden Spike was drilled, one of the owners of the Central Pacific made a bet with one of the owners of the Union Pacific, that the Central Pacific crew could lay ten miles of track in one day. Which was a pretty extraordinary feat. And so, the guy took the bet, and basically, this was one of the most extraordinary militarily precise operations, that anybody had ever seen up until that point. And they literally had an uninterrupted line, a moving line, of 1,000 people on each side of the track as it was being laid, moving at a rate of 1 mile an hour, laying railroad track; and, in fact, about a mile an hour, particularly through that kind of terrain, is about the maximum that you would be able to have an army march—never mind building a railroad. They took a long lunch break of about two hours, at about 1:30 in the afternoon. They started at dawn, and by that point, they knew they were going to achieve it, and then some. And they had back-up crews ready to replace them, and they said, "No, no, no, we're not going to even do it." And so, they completed the whole thing; they laid about ten and a half miles of track in one day.

The guy who lost the bet, welshed on it. He was one of the people who later went to jail for the financial swindles, but, as I say, there were a lot of warts in this project. This was not all done by saints floating on clouds, but it really was a question of leadership.

And I think it's an important question of leadership for everybody here to think about today, since we confront continuously this paradox, of this great opportunity and great mission which we're all confronted with; and we look around and we see a population that's not really ready to fight. But you see that if you had leadership, and provided a certain sense of mission and purpose, that people who have enormous flaws, can change overnight. They may not become perfect citizens of a republic within 24 hours, but you can get a lot of good,

FIGURE 3

The World Land-Bridge, as sketched out by transportation consultant H.A. Cooper. The development corridors of the Eurasian Land-Bridges and their extensions elsewhere in the world, is today's overall development mission, as the Transcontinental was to Abraham Lincoln's United States.

healthy work out of them, and that that's exactly what happened on this project.

Transformation of the United States

So, what happened?

The poet Walt Whitman had traveled west, partly on the Transcontinental Railroad, before it was completed, and then by stage coach and other things, and he wrote a famous book called *Passage to India*. And at the time, everybody thought that the great benefit of the Transcontinental Railroad was going to be trade with the Far East. But what happened is, that in 1869, the same year that the Railroad was completed, so was the Suez Canal, so this Western route proved not to be such an enormously important boost for American trade with the Far East.

But it turned out, that was never going to be the situation anyway. The issue was, that you massively expanded the population of the entire Western half of the United States; you had city-building projects going on everywhere, massive internal trade, many other devel-

opment projects that went on from there. And so what was really important—and this was really understood by Lincoln, and the Careys, and Clay, and others—was the transformation of the United States into the greatest industrial republic on the planet, in a very short period of time, through this extraordinary project, among other things.

Now, this is a fairly good representation of the World Land-Bridge (**Figure 3**). People are familiar with the Eurasian part of it, but the idea of the Eurasian Land-Bridge was in fact implicit—and for many people, explicit—in the Transcontinental Railroad. There were large numbers of Russian military engineers who participated in the building of the Transcontinental Railroad, with the idea that they were going to go back to Russia, and do the same thing there, which you see. After doing this little pipsqueak 2,000-mile line through the middle of nowhere, now you were ready for a real challenge, in the Trans-Siberian Railroad. And it took one generation to complete it.

Twenty-five years after the Transcontinental, the

FIGURE 4
United States: High-Speed Rail Corridor Designations

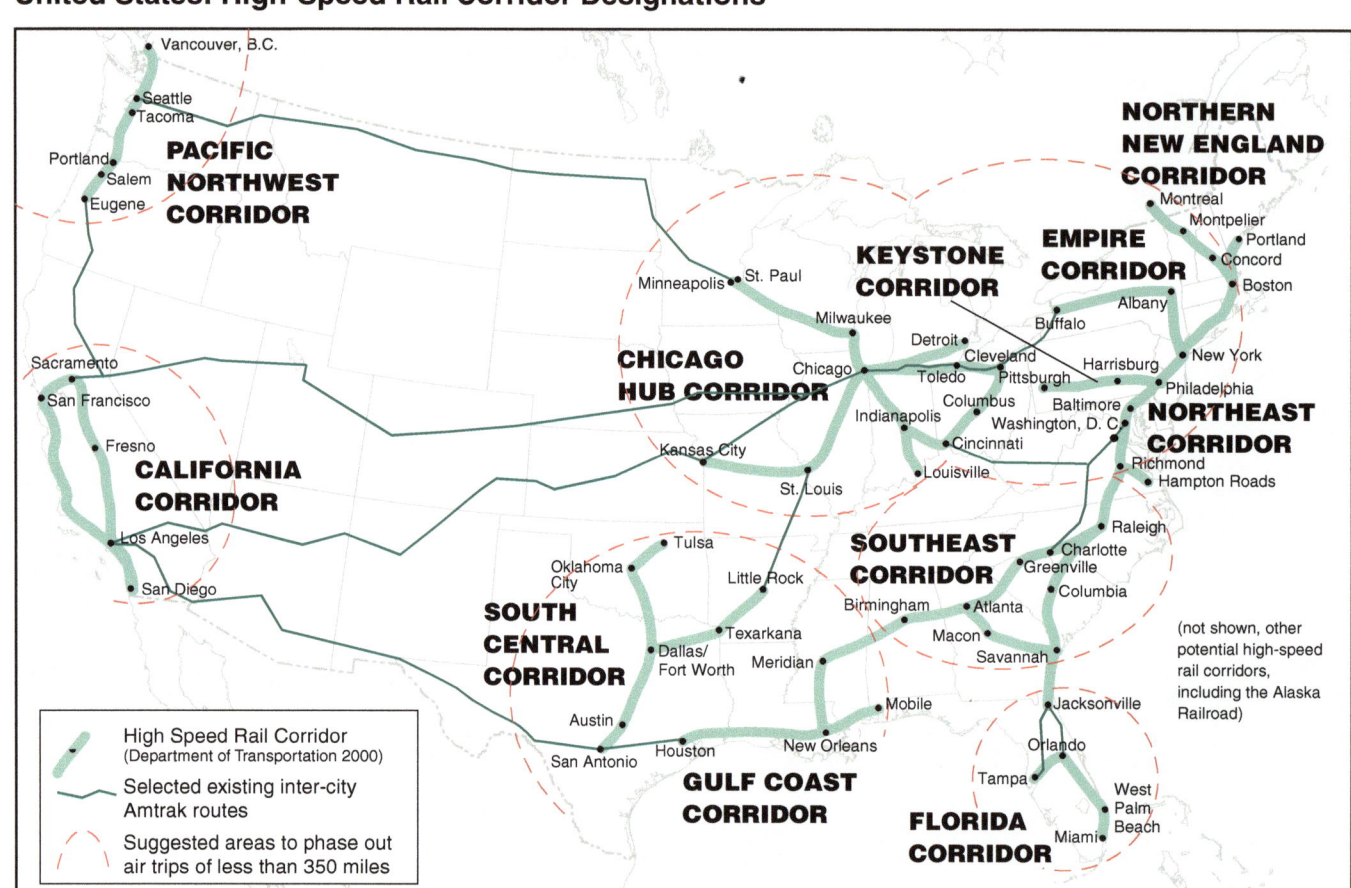

Today: High-speed rail plans unfunded and unrealized. These high-speed rail corridors were named by the Department of Transportation as long ago as 2000, because of local demand; but no intention to build them has emerged under British-agent Presidents Bush and Obama.

Trans-Siberian Railroad was finished; and not only were there American engineers in every phase of the project, but the first locomotive to ride across the Trans-Siberian Railroad was built in Philadelphia by the Baldwin Engine Company.

So this was a global project, in the same way that Lyndon LaRouche talks about the Eurasian Land-Bridge. Nobody thinks about this as a particular project for one country, or one region. It's the mission of global development, and the idea of connecting the entire world, through these high-speed rail lines, which are not merely transportation routes, but development corridors (**Figure 4**). The only economic sense is, every step along the way, to take these barren areas, and turn them into areas of great economic development, using the most advanced technologies of the moment.

So, here we are, 150 years later, we're still talking about railroads. Thank God, we're talking about a whole new generation—really, two generations of technology later. But the principle is the same. So, when some idiot says to you, "What's in it for us? What's all this with these railroads in Asia? What do we need that for?" Or says that this project represents a strategic threat to the United States, then you can just write down their name in the book of members of the Party of Treason, because that's what they are.

Note: Much of the material presented here was based on the book *Nothing Like It in the World—The Men Who Built the Transcontinental Railroad 1863-1869*, by Stephen E. Ambrose (New York, Simon & Schuster, 2000).

The Unclassified Mind: A Scientist Unlocks the Future

by Charles B. Stevens and Paul Gallagher

June 2—The technological advances of the Twentieth Century, "the Nuclear Age," were based on the scientific creativity of the Nineteenth, culminating in the broadly fruitful genius of Albert Einstein and Max Planck.

A leading scientist of the Twentieth Century who was both persistently creative, and strongly motivated by "the common aims of humanity," was also widely attacked by the century's scientific priesthood and before the public.

This was Dr. Edward Teller (1908-2003), the "father of the H-bomb," whose actual life's work was focused ("like a laser," as we have learned to say) on the principle that the completely open, unclassified pursuit of science's creative frontiers is the basis for both peace, and human progress.

He thus became also a father of the Presidential science policy of Ronald Reagan which ended the Cold War—that policy known as the Strategic Defense Initiative (SDI)—and later a father of the Strategic Defense of Earth (SDE) against destructive space objects, now an essential aspect of the science policy of Russia, and a crucial potential for collaboration of American and Russian scientists.

In his earlier work as a nuclear chemist, within Einstein's legacy as mediated to Teller by collaborators of that great genius, Teller helped discover crystalline states which are now making tomorrow's high-temperature superconducting materials, so-called "Jahn-Teller metals."

Ironically, Teller's solitary and unstoppable decision in 1948 to pursue the secrets of "the Super"—a hydrogen-fusion bomb—stemmed from a commitment both to *prevent* nuclear war, and to launch open fusion-energy research competition and collaboration between the United States and the Soviet Union, creating the maximum rate of human progress of which each great power was capable.

Lawrence Livermore National Laboratory

President Reagan gives Edward Teller the National Medal of Science in 1983.

Dr. Teller and Lyndon LaRouche worked separately from the 1970s, to bring about what became known in 1983 as President Reagan's "Star Wars" SDI. But the idea which both had, unique among all advocates of "anti-ICBM defense systems," was that the crash programs on the new physical principles involved in laser-based defense systems should be open, unclassified, and shared between U.S. and Soviet scientific teams.

It was *this* aspect of the President's famous Mar. 23, 1983 televised address announcing the SDI—sharing the research with the Soviets—which shocked and dismayed the cold warriors *of both sides.*

And the Soviet rejection of Reagan's offer, which was also Teller's offer, and which had been the offer directly conveyed to the Russians in advance by LaRouche, powerfully contributed to the Soviet Union's collapse six years later, despite the sabotage of the SDI itself by underfunding, and then non-funding.

'A Qualified Martian'

In remarks in late 2011, during the enthusiasm of *Curiosity*'s landing on Mars, Lyndon LaRouche appreciated Edward Teller's creative generation of "science-driver" policies for Presidents:

> Those among us who have shared some knowledge of the kinds of scientific mission-orientation underlying the launching of the Strategic Defense Initiative (SDI) and kindred missions, who share it more or less immediately, as I do, or as do younger persons committed to this same legacy, can not overlook what I recall as Dr. Edward Teller's leading contributions to what became known by both of us as The Strategic Defense Initiative (SDI). We must also focus a mission-orientation commitment to the defense of Dr. Teller's leading role, in today's crucial goal of defending both the parts, and, ultimately, the whole of our planet Earth against what might be considered, in the rough, as space debris.

> At the same time, we recall with some touches of bitterness, that minds such as those of Max Planck and Albert Einstein point us toward leading thinkers from [their] generation ... who have represented something which tended to become lost in the course of what is recalled as World War I and post-World War II scientific and musical society. Much that had been beautiful as scientific achievement, became relatively mired in the cheap-shot qualities of practice which became all too familiar in the generation educated under post-World War II conditions. In effect, these, my own recollections, must also have often occurred to a qualified Martian such as my ironical sometime critic, Dr. Teller.

> Dr. Teller is remembered with a particular emphasis on the subject of the SDI, and today's increasing concern for the need of means of defense against asteroids which have been, are, or may be deadly threats to large parts of the population of Earth, or, ultimately, worse. Those of my associates now, recognize that a very serious concern is needed against this general threat, especially in light of our stunning lack of knowledge respecting the awesomely great mass of potentially threatening asteroids whose identities we have yet to locate.

> All of this which I have just presented as content within this present chapter of the report, now separates the practice of science prior to *Curiosity*, from the larger category which the success of *Curiosity* has prompted to be recognized as an

entirely new and much greater pathway to be opened now, when the foothold of mankind on Mars has just gained an awesomely greater mission-objective in all conceivable respects.

> The particular mission to which Dr. Teller had devoted particular attention—the threat to man on Earth from asteroids—should be long remembered, together with his famous mustering of efforts on behalf of the Strategic Defense Initiative (SDI), as the quality of humanity in science which the present threat of thermonuclear warfare demands of us all today.

> With that, will come a further, very special concern of my own: the true meaning of the human mind.

'Science Drivers' and War Avoidance

When Edward Teller launched his single-handed campaign for development of the hydrogen-fusion or "thermonuclear" bomb in 1948, he was acting against a policy of continuing the brief 1945 nuclear war against Japan, with a "preventive" nuclear war against Russia. This was the policy of mathematician Bertrand Russell, whom LaRouche has rightly called "the most evil man of the Twentieth Century." Russell set it forth publicly in a chilling article in the *Bulletin of the Atomic Scientists* for Oct. 1, 1946, entitled "The Atomic Bomb and the Prevention of War."

Russell's title was sophistry: The article proposed to publicly threaten, and carry out if "necessary," a nuclear attack on Russia, to "prevent" the Soviet Union from breaking the U.S.-British atomic bomb monopoly. This "Strangelove" policy was agreeable to Harry Truman and to the Manhattan Project's most influential scientist, J. Robert Oppenheimer. It was based on the United States developing a stockpile of hundreds of atomic weapons during the late 1940s, while Russia had none or nearly none, and therefore winning a nuclear war either by a pre-emptive nuclear attack, or by Russian capitulation to the U.S.-British permanent atomic monopoly.

The successful detonation of the Russian atomic bomb in August 1949 in no way interfered with the implementation of the Russell doctrine, since it would take the USSR at least another five years to build a militarily significant stockpile of atom bombs. And General Eisenhower having held back from the Presidency in 1948, Truman was still in office, and ready to wage "preventive" nuclear attacks to which Eisenhower would never have consented.

Crucially, Russell and his co-thinkers were demanding at the same time within the nuclear science community, that thermonuclear fusion research not be pursued at all; that nuclear science end with the fission process.

As Lyndon LaRouche has reviewed in detail, Bertrand Russell and his leading collaborators nearly succeeded in snuffing out science during the 1927 Solvay conference (see Albert Einstein's God). Among Russell's collaborators in this were J. Robert Oppenheimer and I.I. Rabi, who together are credited with bringing the "New Physics"—the anti-Einstein, anti-Planck so-called quantum physics—to the United States. This Russellite no-science policy was rescinded for a brief period in 1939, with the British support for the Manhattan Project to meet the Nazi danger. But with the end of World War II, the zero-science policy was re-implemented. Teller's 1949 crash fusion program was opposed.

U.S. National Archives

Hiroshima, after the August 6, 1945 dropping of the atomic bomb.

Teller, in the midst of the buildup for such a "preventive" nuclear war, launched a drive in 1948 for development of the far more powerful H-bomb—open-ended science, as he did not then know how such a fusion weapon could be made. It was also a mobilization, in the ranks of nuclear scientists, for a crash thermonuclear fusion program, as a science driver for technological progress. Most of the atomic scientists who, like Teller, were most enthusiastic to pursue thermonuclear fusion for endless energy for mankind, had also tried to stop the Hiroshima and Nagasaki bombings, and were in an uproar against Russell's preventive nuclear war proposal.

And they shared an opposition to classification of nuclear science work—weapons work included—in which Teller was to show himself bolder than any other over the next 40 years.

During World War II before Nagasaki and Hiroshima, Dr. Teller had brought the scientists' circular letter of his mentor, James Franck, to Los Alamos Scientific Laboratory.

Franck was a chemist colleague of William Draper Harkins, and those two had published a paper relating Einstein's famous general relativity equation, $E=mc^2$, to thermonuclear fusion energy, back in 1915. Teller wrote of Franck:

Professor Franck was one of the two or three people who had the deepest influence on my own scientific development. I learned from him not only that most of the important things in physics cannot be described in a nonmathematical language, but also that mathematics is being used all too often to obscure the essentially simple character of the underlying ideas.[1]

The letter/petition Teller brought from Franck to Los Alamos in 1945, was a proposal to first carry out a nonlethal demonstration of the atomic bomb, for example, by exploding it high above Tokyo Bay, or in other ways demonstrating its power to Japanese leaders without attacking their people with it. J. Robert Oppenheimer, director at Los Alamos, intercepted the Franck letter before Teller could circulate it, and lied to Teller that "that much wiser people than ourselves in Washington" were seriously considering these options. Actually, as Dr. Teller learned much later to his great dismay, Oppenheimer led the Scientific Advisory Panel of the Interim Committee that forcefully put through the Churchill-Truman policy over senior military officers' objections: no demonstration; rather, nuclear attacks on cities.

Thus Dr. Teller's first attempt to prevent the use of nuclear weapons, along with such as James Franck and Dr. Robert Moon who organized "Concerned Scientists" at the Chicago Manhattan Project base, failed.

But Teller's second effort was, ironically, his push

<hr>

1. Univ. of Chicago Special Collections, James Franck Collection, Box 24, Folder 23, Edward Teller notes in 1965.

for development of the hydrogen-fusion bomb in 1948, when the very influential Russell was organizing for a "preventive" nuclear attack on Russia.

In the narrowest sense, any significant weapons-design effort based on hydrogen thermonuclear fusion would require large-scale production of tritium, the heaviest isotope of hydrogen. This would immediately distract from the production of fissile fuel for the atom bomb stockpile required by Russell's plan.

More importantly, the possibility of an H-bomb could completely undermine the Russellite preventive-war strategy. Technically, even one thermonuclear fusion hydrogen bomb could have the firepower of a thousand "atomic" or fission bombs. Russia, to be specific, could transform overnight a militarily insignificant handful of atom bombs into a powerful nuclear deterrent.

Teller was thus demonstrating one of his core beliefs as a scientist—that classification, even the intensely compartmentalized classification of the Manhattan Project, was as fruitless as it was wrong: If a "super" could be done, Soviet scientists would do it. Russell's preventive war, therefore, was a recipe for absolute disaster for humanity.

The deeper question was whether unfettered scientific thinking would be permitted, to discover "science drivers" for human progress: Whether science which looked to the future, would survive the Twentieth Century and the supremacy of "mathematicians" like Russell who pronounced human knowledge to be arbitrary, and human population dangerous to the Earth.

Teller's primary goal was to develop new science and technology for the benefit of all humankind. Later, in a public speech in 1966, he estimated that thermonuclear and nuclear science and technology had advanced to the ability to support a human population of more than 30 billion at a modern standard of living. This had been the personal "driver" of his late 1940s campaign: to develop thermonuclear fusion—the decades-earlier vision of Einstein's collaborators—as the open-ended scientific leader for human technology.

'Open Laboratories'

The effort to develop the hydrogen-fusion bomb, "fathered" by Dr. Teller, opened one broad road toward fusion power: inertial confinement or "laser" fusion. The first laser was not invented until 1960 and was then of very low power. But Teller's discovery a decade earlier, for the H-bomb, showed how laser fusion would occur. His *hohlraum* design (a German word meaning "hollow chamber") effectively made the high-power

Academician Evgeny Velikhov, Teller's frequent interlocutor, is today president of Russia's National Research Center at the Kurchatov Institute.

iter.org

x-rays from the detonation of fission explosives packed around the hydrogen-ion fuel, into a tuned "soft x-ray" pulse, which compressed and heated the hydrogen-ion fuel into a far more massive fusion explosion.

After the H-bomb was developed, Teller threw himself into fusion power research in both the magnetic confinement and inertial confinement fields. What distinguished him was his attitude to the leaders of Soviet research in the field. Though his *hohlraum* design was deeply classified, he and his colleagues at the Lawrence Livermore Laboratory had public exchanges about it with leading Soviet researchers. Teller's belief was that Soviet knowledge in the field was, in the nature of science, every bit as advanced as his own, and that progress required "open laboratories" (his phrase) and a competition to develop the technological fruits of this "military" science.

In November 1976, Dr. Teller and the chief of the U.S. Magnetic Fusion Research effort, Edwin Kintner held, together with the leading figure in Soviet fusion research, Academician Evgeny P. Velikhov, a session at the American Nuclear Society annual meeting in Washington, D.C., on how to organize fusion research as the science driver for the common aims of humanity. The abstract of the discussion, given to the scientific media, said:

Optimism is expressed on the prospects for success in practical fusion power by the end of this century. Controlled thermonuclear fusion through inertial confinement, magnetic confinement in Tokamaks, systems using lasers, relativistic electron beams, and magnetic fields are reviewed. Recent achievements in plasma heating and confinement are surveyed. Terawatt-output lasers, superconducting magnets, advanced materials, vacuum pumps, feedback control, and improvements in targets, power sources, and fuelling are considered.

Seven years later in August 1983—just a few months following the shock of President Reagan's announcement of the SDI and offer of U.S.-Soviet scientific cooperation in developing defenses against nuclear ICBMs—Teller and Velikhov had another public meeting at the "Third International Conference on Nuclear War" in Erice, Italy. Despite the Soviet Politburo leadership's animus against SDI, and public fury against both Teller and LaRouche, Dr. Teller and Academician Velikhov agreed to jointly propose a U.S.-Russian magnetic confinement fusion experiment to be set up in Moscow.

Teller spoke of the "common aims of humanity" as being the aims of the SDI which he had promoted: Not merely the prospect of ending Mutually Assured Destruction with beam-weapon defenses against ICBMs, but the prospects of curing diseases, digging canals, transforming human communications, and exploring the galaxy with the "relativistic beam"

technologies which would be developed.

LaRouche organized major conferences of scientific and military leaders all over Europe, in Japan, and in South America, and in the United States in 1984 and 1985, whose subject was precisely this idea.

Teller began, later that decade, to develop the idea of *planetary defense* (i.e., against the threat of devastation by asteroids) based on the same scientific work driving fusion research broadly, and the SDI. When the Berlin Wall fell at the end of that decade, proposals began to come from the Russian side for "open laboratories" for U.S.-Russian-European common work on science and technology for planetary defense.

This scientific cooperation—looking far to the future and far removed from what appear as "practical considerations" to most people—is today a major aspect of Russian science policy, under the rubric of "Strategic Defense of Earth." The Erice, Italy conferences with which Dr. Teller and Lawrence Livermore Laboratories were deeply involved, became the annual "International Seminars on Nuclear War and Planetary Emergencies."

Erice 1983: Reaching Out To the Soviets

An international conference in Erice, Sicily in late August 1983, was the occasion for Edward Teller to strike a major blow for U.S.-Soviet cooperation to develop strategies to prevent nuclear war. At the conclusion of the conference, Teller for the United States, Prof. Evgeny Velikhov for the Soviet Union, and Prof. Antonino Zichichi for Europe, signed a document which created a commission of 100 U.S. and Soviet scientists, dedicated to investigating the feasibility of defensive beam-weapons development, and to conducting a computer analysis on the effects of nuclear war.

Significant excerpts from the final communiqué, as published by the Rome daily *Il Tempo* August 24, under the headline "No to Deterrence Doctrine: The Erice Document," follow:

- The mutual exchange of ideas, data, and information, which resulted from the three sessions of the Eric international seminars on nuclear warfare, are of greatest importance for us.

- The previous sessions opened the path to new investigations of the global effects of a U.S.-U.S.S.R. nuclear clash, the results of which were discussed here in a climate of scientific rigor, and therefore objectively.... Such studies should be developed further with greater collaboration on an international scale....

- Another important point emerged during this third session, and is precisely the problem of defensive weapons. The underlying philosophy of this new point lies in the problem of studying the possibility of identifying new means for getting out of the present balance of terror. The first of these means is the reduction of nuclear arms. The second is the idea of new defensive weapons....

- It is therefore proposed to form a joint Europe-U.S.-U.S.S.R. research group, based at the Ettore Majorana center, for collaborative study of two above-mentioned points: 1) The simulation and evaluation of the global consequences of a U.S.-U.S.S.R. nuclear conflict. 2) A way out of the present balance of terror; and in particular, if it is possible to conceive of a new type of defense system against nuclear destruction.

The Current Presidential Transition Period

This discussion took place between Lyndon LaRouche and participants in the LaRouchePAC activists' conference call May 28, 2015. The call, in which more than 500 people took part, was hosted by John Ascher.

John Ascher: Good evening, everyone. This is John Ascher here in Leesburg, Va., welcoming everyone back to our second "Fireside Chat" with Lyndon LaRouche....

Lyndon LaRouche: Well, we got a little problem that got dumped in my lap early this evening. Barbara Boyd gave a report and a recommendation: What has happened is that there was an operation by adversary forces, and some of us were trying to find out who the adversary forces were, and why they were doing it, and how they were doing it. Quite recently we were able to pinpoint those forces who were active and who were effectively weakening the financial resources of our organization here.

So Barbara Boyd, who of course is the relevant person in this area, for managing of finances and so forth, has suggested that what we have to do, in order to deal with this problem. We have to try to raise some funds, within the organization and from it, in order to try to beat off some of the really deadly threats, financial threats, which are hitting in this area. So they asked me to say something about it, and I said I will say something about it.

I'll make a comment on this thing, too, because it's very significant: The issue, which Barbara doesn't say explicitly, but she did say on other occasions, earlier, was that we had a group of people who were operating as former, or allegedly former, members of our organization, and these people were all without doubt determined, factually, to be all actually agents of enemy forces; some of them had been people who were recruited from our organization, and were otherwise using things to try to do damage to us, especially in the Leesburg area. In other areas, we don't have any specific problem of that type, on our registration, yet; but in this area, we've had for several months, a trend which was an outsides-forces' meddling. And more recently, we've been able to determine that more precisely.

So that's the point: some of the people affected by this thing, are saying we need to raise some direct money, quickly, for the general organization and from it, in order to stave off a present emergency crisis. And that's her report, which she said to me late this afternoon. And I think the thing that she's saying is quite appropriate in a sense, but the point is, it's our organization, the members here, for example, participating now, who will have to judge how they want to approach this, but I think it's something we have to do. I don't know how we're going to do it; Barbara said explicitly, she doesn't know how she's going to do it. And so I think this is the way we have to look at it.

Anyway, I think otherwise, apart from that little piece of bad news, I think we're ready to go.

Q: This is B— from South Florida, and I was fortunate enough to hear last week's call, and fortunately enough, there were so many good questions I didn't get on last week. But I did contact the activists in Leesburg in regards to it, and I would just love to hear Lyndon LaRouche's response to this: We have the Greek default with the IMF and the EU coming up June 5, and I think that it's perfect timing to demand Glass-Steagall be pushed, rammed through, before July 4th, when July 5th is the actual, legal default, on June 5th, of Greece. Because as the EU will start collapsing, there are quite a few countries, I understand, that want

National Archives

President Franklin Roosevelt signs Glass-Steagall into law, June 16, 1933.

only one man, as a qualified scientist, who was ever supported. And guess who? Albert Einstein. No other so-called scientist, was actually honestly competent as a scientist during the course of the 20th Century.

And after the 20th Century had passed, and we were passing into the present century, things have gotten worse at an accelerated rate.

And Glass-Steagall is a pivot: not only the content of Glass-Steagall, but Glass-Steagall as an essential instrument of the policy of returning to the economic policies of our Presidency, that is, of the United States. If you don't push Glass-Steagall, and go from the start of it, you're not going to save this nation. You're not going to save our people. So Glass-Steagall is indispensable: There can be no substitute for Glass-Steagall. Anyone who doesn't agree on Glass-Steagall, is either mentally ill, or very much confused.

to get out the door along with Greece; the United States would be wise, in my opinion, to ram through Glass-Steagall before July 4th, to protect her nation's assets. And I would love to hear any remarks, ideas, responses.

LaRouche: Okay, it's rather simple. Of course, Glass-Steagall is absolutely indispensable. If you don't include Glass-Steagall in reforming the system, you're not going to accomplish anything, because all the other features of the system would fail to meet the requirement now.

Now, let me just explain one thing about this, which is not generally taken up by our discussions, but they very much occupy my views on these matters: We're in a situation, where we entered the 20th Century—now people say, that's a long time ago. Yeah, that year, and from there on. In the 19th Century, you still had some of the greatest qualities of genius being generated in the trans-European area, the most famous names.

What happened was, that with the beginning of the 20th Century—that is, the year 1900 and 1901, that period—since that time, the moral and intellectual capabilities of the people of Europe, but particularly the United States, have been in a constant rate of decline. For example, in the whole 20th Century, there was

Go Back to a Science-Driver Program

Q: It's L— from Albany, [N.Y.] and we were lobbying for Glass-Steagall at the [State] Capitol last Wednesday, so we're very much committed.

I think the other thing that, really, I'm also concerned about, is how to generate jobs and manufacturing. I drove through Gary, Ind., and it's a ghost town. And I am old enough to know what we were like when we produced the cars, and—in fact, we'd invent the thing, and then China's making it right now. I need to know how to generate jobs in this country now.

LaRouche: What we have to do essentially is very simple: We have to go back to the idea of a science-driver program, as the basis for the entire economy of the United States, that is, for everything that the United States represents as an economy. Glass-Steagall is an expression of that absolutely, indispensable mode. It's always been the case. It doesn't mean we've always had that case, but anytime we were doing the right things, we did follow that case. And right now, if you don't have Glass-Steagall, you cannot solve any of the problems of the United States.

And you have to realize this, that the United States has been degenerating, over the course of the 20th Century, and is still going in that direction today. So that, if

creative commons/Khalidshou

China's high-speed train leaving the Shanghai station

you don't get the package, of which Glass-Steagall is a characteristic feature, you're not going to save this nation.

We are now headed for Hell, economically, and also, there's a plan now in play with the water question, which is being pushed in California and elsewhere. Now, what this governor of California is doing, is committing genocide against not only the people of California, but this is now extended to a broader area of the Western states. And on the edge, the rest of the United States area is now about to get into the same kind of problem.

There are solutions for this problem, but the governor of California is not going to allow that to happen—unless we sort of get him out of the picture. But that's where we are.

Q: This is G— from Washington State. I'd like to ask Mr. LaRouche if he would help with the promotion of Franklin Roosevelt's Columbia Basin project as a national project, and if he would help assign the people to help me on the promotion of that.

LaRouche: Yes, yes. But that's just a generalization when said that way. There are very specific approaches to carrying that out, and what is necessary is to go into a discussion of what those specific approaches are. The basic thing is, that the human species realizes itself as being human, only through the creative powers of the human individual mind, the human mind in general.

Now, let's take, for example, right now: We allegedly have a great water crisis in the United States, and the West Coast, of course, is the leading subject on this matter currently. But those people say, "We can't do this, we can't do that, because we're running out water." Now the fact of the matter is, we are not running out of water! The supply of water is not located merely in the Earth area; as a matter of fact, the Earth area is a relatively small part of the total water supply which the United States, for example, and other nations and so forth, have available to them.

The basic system, for the water system of the United States, is merely a part of a much more powerful system called the "galactic system." In point of fact, the existence of humanity depends upon factors of the galactic system, of which the water supply is the most obvious. And the struggle now is to get people to understand, how to get the "juice," shall we say, out of the galactic area, which is there waiting for us: How do we tap into that, and bring it into play to solve our problems. And the future of mankind depends entirely, on the promotion of that revolution.

It is a perfectly feasible revolution; it has a precisely scientific set of characteristics. It's this thing which follows work of Kepler, the great Kepler, who was the first person to understand how the galactic system was created. He didn't have a complete view of the galactic system, but now that system is known, the galactic principle is known; and it's also known that the water on Earth depends upon the management programs prescribed for the galaxy, not the local water system.

And so, if we go at that kind of problem, that kind of thinking, which is quite feasible—it's not easy. It's difficult to get through the process, because it requires a lot of steps of work, in order to get mankind to really realize what the water system is. But we have already existing *for us now*, we have the access to the kind of

Senator Rand Paul, May 20, 2015

CSPAN

technology, which is known technology, that is, in terms of the system. And all we have to do, is get a little smarter, and learn how to apply ourselves to that.

A Good Presidential System

Q: Hello, this is J— from Michigan. And my question is, the voter fraud with the electronic voting still going on. Now the Democrats are controlling that, and so, how do we get a hold of this? I can agree with you, if we just go back to just a single ballot, to get a fair election.

LaRouche: Well, I think you've got an option is coming up this Saturday: It's called [Martin] O'Malley. Now, I've gone through the list of candidates that are known to me, that is, all the present candidates for election, known to me presently.

Now, this guy, O'Malley is right now, the only probable case of a candidate qualified to lead the nation in solving our problems. Without that kind of approach, the approach he represents, we don't have much of a chance, in the United States, for our people. And we don't have anybody else on the job right now, who is committed to O'Malley's position, as a Presidential candidate.

I also look around the issue, and I find the other guys who are considered Presidential candidates, they're not all bad people—that's not the point. But they do not have the kind of commitment that's needed.

It's just like what happened in the 20th Century. We had all these guys who were called scientists, and there was only one scientist in the 20th Century who was really competent: Einstein. The rest of them were all a little bit kooky, and were not really up to the job. So the issue now is, do we know that? Well, we do know some of that material, we do have some insight into that.

And O'Malley so far has indicated that he's a man who's committed in that direction. Now, I can't guarantee him; I don't have that kind of insight. But I do have a good idea of what he's been doing, and I understand how he's operating. And what I understand more than anything else, is all the other ones are no good! They're not necessarily bad people; they just can't do the job which we desperately need to be done!

And so, I would say, we should encourage O'Malley. And we're looking for a Presidential candidacy which, in practice, can deliver an organization of leading political forces inside the United States, regroup those forces, and bring them into unified play. That is, create a real Presidential system, of the type that we have done a number of times, in the U.S. history.

But that's what we require. We have to get a Presidential system: You need a good President, otherwise you don't get a good Presidential system. But we need a Presidential system, a President who can represent that. And that is our best shot—for everything.

Q: Hi Lyn, this is A— from the Bronx. Lyn, earlier today, I received an e-mail from the organization of the 28pages.org. They're announcing that Rand Paul [Republican] and [Ron] Wyden, Democrat, two Senators, will be introducing a resolution to the Senate next week, joined by [former Sen. Bob] Graham and members of the House that have put that Resolution[1] forward, and that this would be happening on June 2.

Now, I don't want to get too excited about this. We know that these things can get stuck, but I was wondering, because this is from the Saudis to the British, to the outtake of Obama, this could seemingly happen very quickly. So I was wondering if you could tell us what your thoughts are? And what we should be doing in New York, to get people like [Sen. Chuck] Schumer, who should know better, to support this resolution?

LaRouche: I think you know Schumer needs a little

---

1. A Resolution to declassify the suppressed 28 pages of the Joint Congressional Inquiry on 9/11 dealing with the role of Saudi Arabia.

bit more encouragement, because he has not had much encouragement recently under the present President. So that has to be taken into account.

But on the Rand Paul thing: Rand Paul has a very specific feature in his program which is prominent at this time. Now, I don't know about Rand Paul's policies in the broad sense. In other words, I couldn't give him A marks, 100% marks, all the way up and down. That I can't do. But I do know, that what he has committed himself to, as stated, is something which is absolutely valid. It's not the shebang, it's not everything, but it's an element, which when—well, let me just put my answer to your question this way:

Look, the creation of a Presidential system, which is in accord with the best practice of our system of Presidency, requires a broad team of people, gathered around a figure we call "the President." But there are many people who have to contribute to make up the combined effect, which represents the kind of President we need. We need a Chief Executive, yes; and the Chief Executive has to be a good choice. But the efficiency with which the good choice can be realized, depends upon bringing a team together, around that Presidential candidate. That is what we must do, and therefore Rand Paul is one of the figures you're going to look at, right now, and say, "Rand Paul, are you really real?" Because I think a lot of people in the United States are looking at candidates, and looking about them, and saying, "Is this guy really real?"

And I think Rand Paul, at least on this score, and his behavior on this score, is rather real. He's doing good things, and what he's doing—what he's not doing, I'm not sure about—but what he's doing in the case right now, is good.

What we need, however, is to create a Presidential system, and a Presidential system is not *a* President; very rarely can *a* President be successful, even if they're the best quality. You need a best President, a best option; but you also need a combination of people, whose combined talents, brought together in the proper way, give you a real Presidency, something like Franklin Roosevelt did.

White House/Pete Souza

Obama in the Oval Office with Vice President Biden, March 4, 2015

Remove Obama To Prevent Nuclear War

Q: This is K—. I just want to say, Lyn, I thank you for your service, and your truth-telling throughout the years. And I just wanted to get your take on the situation concerning Ukraine, and Donetsk, and Putin, and the constant ceasefire, and the breaking of the ceasefire, and the United States role in backing the Ukraine government, and also the situation in the South China Sea, with the surveillance planes and China's continuing to warn the U.S., and this constant escalation—which could lead into a thermonuclear situation. I just wanted to get your take on it.

LaRouche: Absolutely, you got my attention.

The point is, like the China Sea situation—we must get rid of Obama. We must impeach this guy, throw him out now. This is not an idea of replacing him, or waiting for the next President. You've got to remove Obama right now. We've got to find the members of Congress, and so forth, who have the guts to do that.

What you're looking at, *if* Obama were to succeed in what he's doing, the direction he's going, you're going to be, very soon, in a thermonuclear war, from which we don't know who could survive, if anyone. So, therefore, *Obama must be slugged out of his position.* Because as long as he's there, and with his evil intentions—and I can say frankly, his evil intentions—you haven't got a chance. So this guy has to be ushered from office. And we have to have at least an emergency replacement, which may not be perfect; which may have a lot of faults; but we've got to get rid of this threat of a global thermonuclear war.

Because if such a war breaks out, and if a war of that type breaks out, we will *have* a thermonuclear war. And the chances of survival of the human species on this planet, is very limited. I'm not talking about something long-term. I'm talking about something very short-term. We are already on the edge. With Obama as President,

parliament.uk

Queen Elizabeth, accompanied by His Royal Virus Prince Philip, addresses opening of Parliament, May 27.

we are already on the edge of the extinction of the United States, the people of the United States—and other people, in other parts of the world as well.

Q: This is K— from New York. I have been reading that Russia wants to destroy our grid. I have been reading that ISIS wants to destroy our grid. I don't think Russia would benefit by it, but ISIS likes to destroy, and that's all they want to do. If that happens, is this Tesla electrical system something that could be used to replace what we have now, really quickly, and do you have people who give thought to this?

LaRouche: It's a reasonable question, but I think I would approach it in a different way.

Yes, as long as we have this situation—remember that the policy is that of the British Empire. In modern times, our chief enemy has always been the British Empire. The British Empire is the enemy of civilization, in general. Even uncivilized people are victims of the British Empire—that's not a usual fact.

So what the problem is: We must remove those factors in international policy, which mean the threatened extinction of the human species. And the threatened extinction of the human species is something you have to talk about, when you hear the name of Obama. You also have to know, realize, that the British Empire is the chief force of evil on this planet, and has been that for a very long time. And therefore what we need to do, is take that into consideration.

Now, what are the alternatives? We have a thing called BRICS, parts of the planet Earth. China is one of those cases. China is a leading force, a positive force as

a leading force, on the planet right now. It has a greatness which is absolutely amazing. India is now, despite the great starvation, the heat wave and so on, a great nation; it's organized as a great nation. There are other parts of the planet, some parts in South America, some other parts of the planet, which are very good places.

Russia right now is a good place. It's not perfected, but you have to look at its history and see what it's trying to crawl back out of, and then you understand it.

What we need to do: We're going into a new idea of mankind. It's not exactly a change of the old way. But we know now that nations cannot just live with arbitrary attitudes toward other nations. Let the nations live their own way, *but* let's find a way of concert, of bringing our intentions together, one nation to another. Let us have different tastes; that's all right. What we want to do is learn by working together, as nations.

We start from what we think is best for our nation, and we hope the other nation will do the same thing. We may all be wrong, but not perfectly wrong. But we will, in this process, learn how to converge on things which the future of mankind requires. And of course our United States is actually, as created, by people like Alexander Hamilton and his leadership—that's the model. For me, that's the model. It's the best model.

The problem is, we had a bunch of bum Presidents, and they were brought in largely by the influence of the British Empire. Manhattan, for example. Manhattan is actually one of the greatest things in the United States, despite all the bad things that go on in Manhattan. And I can tell you, I know those bad things that are done in Manhattan. *But*, we have within Manhattan, we have an intention in part of the population, which radiates into the best features of New York State. We know other parts of the nation, our nation, which similarly, would like to go in that same direction.

So, the way we have to approach it is that. We have to say, well, we've got to decide what the bad things are. And we've got to recognize what the shortcomings are, apart from the bad things. And we have to bring about a set of relations among nations, where the nations

"The Torches of Nero," by Henryk Siemiradzki, 1877

will live at peace with one another, while looking at their common mistakes, and trying to correct them. That's the history of mankind. It's called progress. And the principle has to be the principle of progress.

The British System Should Not Exist

Q: This is D— in California. I just wanted to thank you, Lyndon LaRouche, and your organization for phenomenal success in leadership. It's really—it couldn't come at a better time. I have sort of a bifurcated question. I saw the Queen of England speak in front of her House of Lords and Parliament, and she said that her government is going to write a Bill of Rights for the United Kingdom. Since the English, as far as I can tell, wrote the Magna Carta, and the [American] Bill of Rights is based on the Magna Carta, didn't they already have some mind, or the will, to write a Bill of Rights? Why the change? And then, the bifurcated part is: I'm also wondering why she is looking forward to her visit to Germany next month.

LaRouche: The point is ... the legacy. The British Monarchy has not been a good thing. The complications are that some of the Scots are not so bad, some of the Irish are not so bad. But the problem is that the British *system* is, as in Shakespeare's account of the history of England, a pretty good picture of what the problem has been. Also, it means that the creation of the British Empire as such, has been nothing but a pestilence, a pestilence to mankind.

The British System, as an imperial system, should

not exist, because there's no way that you can have a good system if the current monarchy, or the traditional monarchy, continues. And therefore, the problem is exactly that. The problem lies not with the English people, not with the Scots and not with the Irish. The fact is, they are slaves of a certain kind. They don't *have* their own rights, they don't *have* their own abilities. They are simply tools, and they're trying to survive in the role of being the tools they've been made to be.

I know a lot of those people from Britain; my age enables me to know that. And I draw a conclusion on that basis. Often, I find many British citizens—English, Scottish, and so forth—I find they're evil. As a matter of fact, I've got some ancestors out of that breed, so I can't be too afraid about those guys.

But the point is, the British Empire, the monarchy system, as an existent, since the founding of the United States, in particular, is something we want the planet to be free of. And the sooner it goes, the better.

Q: The question is essentially around what was just said, that the Britons are tools of an imperial system—that is what is basic, and the question is, are the words "Roman" and "British" covers for the priestly bank hegemons, or the imperial Israel bank Khazars? Are the words "Roman" and "British" covers, and if they're covers, is a more accurate description, the Vatican Empire? Is the Israel bank Khazar a proxy...?

Ascher: I think she was asking about the relationship between the Roman Empire and the British Empire. It was very faint, but that was the basic question.

LaRouche: I think the evil is about the same. I think the Romans were better at mass killing and slaughter. We have a less bad situation. But the British system has been the most cruel, the most evil system on the planet, for all people. You could take cannibals—you might be able to make excuses for cannibals, but you could never make excuses for the British Empire.

Q: Lyn, thank you for your work. I'm an activist. My name is K— and I'm from West Virginia. One thing that bugs me a lot is the lawlessness in our government. The highest office, like Obama in office, is always disobeying the Constitution, but many of the elected officials underneath him are also the same way. And they don't seem to live by the laws of the land, and they come up and say, "Go." I think this is probably the second-most important issue going on in our country today, excluding the Glass-Steagall.

I recently heard from a Senator's office that Obama is about to be impeached, but it's going to happen very quickly. Can you comment on the lawlessness, and on the hearsay that I heard about Obama being impeached very quickly?

LaRouche: Well, in short, Obama is a disaster. He's a disaster for the United States. Every day he lives right now, is another day of disaster for many people of the United States. And the problem is also, more broadly, what's happened in terms of, for example, the system of the Congress, as such—these institutions that we were so proud of at one point, have broken down. Like that of Franklin Roosevelt, for example, one of our most famous achievers in history. We don't have those around any more.

And the reason we don't have them is because the system of government, as it's managed, doesn't *allow*

EIR's September 5, 2003 issue featured Arnie Schwarzenegger's 2002 consultations with Warren Buffet (left) and Lord Jack Rothschild (right), conducted at Rothschild's English estate prior to Schwarzenegger's election as governor of California.

good Presidents to occur. I've known some good Presidents personally. I've admired some of work they've done. Some of them were of fairly recent vintage. But if you come to a Bush, I would think of burning Bushes—a bad smell, essentially. We've had many Presidents who were bad, really evil. Most of them were British agents.

For example, the Bush family. Prescott Bush was an advocate of Hitler's policy. And certainly he was still living when his sons came along, and they got to be known as the Bushes of the Presidency. And we got a result from the Bushes of the followers of Prescott Bush, which has been pretty much a benchmark of the evil that has occurred to the United States since that time—essentially that period.

So, what we have is a system of Presidency which has some good Presidents in it, but somehow the Presidency itself fails to function. Certain Presidents I know of, they were good persons, and good Presidents, but somebody else was in the woodwork, and destroying and corrupting all the good things.

And that's been the case. Obama is probably the worst President on record in the United States. That's a good example of that. But all the Bushes are very bad. They've always been very bad, and as bad as stupidity can make them.

The Galactic Principle Can Save California

Q: E— out here in Southern California. Lyn, it's a pleasure. Lyndon, I have a question. I've been listening to several of the recent discussions over the phone over the last month or so, and I'm bewildered because it appears to me that, relative to the drought that you cited here in California, that, on the one hand, it doesn't appear that LaRouche and company are acknowledging that humans are the underlying problem, or that humans, by changing their behavior, represent a part of the formula for the solution to it.

When we have, for example, the burning of the jungles in South America, the impact that that has had on the Northern Hemisphere is a rather documented scientific fact, and yet, I hear about these galactic solutions, which seem to be rather ambiguous at best. I thought you may be able to comment upon that.

LaRouche: Well, there's nothing wrong about the galactic solutions, if they are solutions. That's obvious.

The problem has been that mankind in a primitive condition, tends to be a destructive force for mankind. That progress, as such, real progress, the evolution of man's skills, the scientific progress, these things are essential. And these are the things that make mankind different than beasts. So therefore, there are certain things that are essential. Progress, scientific progress, and so forth is absolutely essential.

For example, without a galactic system, you are not going to have a successful population of California! Because with the present trend, which is going into a long trend—and if we sit there and just watch with California, and don't *change* it in the needed way, by applying galactic principles to the galaxy, California is dead. Because it will be a long time before the terrritory called California today, will come back.

So, therefore, progress is essential. And the progress of man, and man's ability to make the changes... For example, what's the problem with the water system in California? Well, two things. First of all, what was good beforehand, when the previous governor of California was there [Gov. Pat Brown (1959-67)]—but after the Apeman [Arnold Schwarzenegger] got in there, and some other people, California shot itself to death by bad governors. And that's the recent case.

But on the broader thing, the problem is, we do need to go to scientific progress, scientific progress. But the problem is, that in the 20th Century, the economy of the United States has been degenerating at a rapid rate.

Library of Congress

Cotton Mather's "Essays To Do Good" used to be a touchstone of American culture before its 20th-Century decline.

Look at the condition of your people in the United States here. What's their condition? Comparative to what the condition had been earlier, the United States and the people of the United States are in the worst condition they could possibly be in, up to this time. Oh yes, they had spare times before, but they don't have any progress any more.

Our own people are insane. Our children, in the 20th Century, school children, and products of school education, are becoming more and more worthless, in terms of their powers to accomplish things. They don't know what to do. Look at the condition of our labor force today. What condition are they living in? What kinds of life are they living? How much better was life 20 years ago, 30 years, 40 years, 50 years ago? Everything is much, much worse than then.

Why? Because we didn't continue progress. But the problem is, you've got to use *real* progress, not imitation progress.

Creating a Leadership

Q: Good evening. This is D— in Berkeley Springs, W.Va. I have a simple question; I'd like to elaborate just a little bit on it. How do we actually get this guy out of office? What are the steps we have to take?

Last year, my wife and I—in fact, it was K—, who spoke to you a few minutes ago—we had two different copies of articles of impeachment that we tried to present to Members of Congress, and nobody had the gonads to even talk about the subject. The only encouragement we had recently was, when we talked to one of the staff members of Sen. Joe Manchin, our Senator, and he said, impeachment is going to happen; it's going to happen, and it's going to happen quickly. Does he know something we haven't heard about yet?

LaRouche: I think the intention is for that to happen. I think what you're having is, the O'Malley candidacy, which is coming up on Saturday, it could be a turning point. That is, it could be a turning point, not because it's a question of whether he's reluctant and so forth to do what he's promising, but the point is, he might be prevented from doing it. Whereas, I've watched this thing carefully: O'Malley is, on the scale of things, the most prominent figure who might save this nation, as President.

Now, that would mean he would have to have some—not just himself; he would have to have a team. Because a single person as President is not a very effective person. Because the other guys may be going in the other direction. But the point is, we have the possibility of winning this thing. What it takes, it takes what's sometimes called guts. But guts is a crude word, and it may not really tell you the real story.

The real story is: Are you enabling and encouraging our citizens to do the kinds of things that will produce the kind of results you want? I think we can do it. I know we can do it, because I've seen it being done before. Our problem has not been that we were a failure; the problem is, we let people get into power, like the Bushes, the Bush family; we let those kinds of bums in the 20th Century, we let them run this place for a while. And I could tell you some things about the Bushes that would terrify you—but it's all true.

So, therefore, the problem is, we have to have, always, two things: guts, and the teamwork to create a leadership, a political leadership, a practical leadership, inside the United States. And we have to pull people together and get them to decide they're going to stick together for that mission. And I think we might get lucky. Because, if you look at what's happening in South America, if you look what's happening in China, if you look what's happening in India, looking at other places like that—progress is keeping progress. It's here.

And it's here on a good part of the planet. The majority of the planet wants progress. And we can pull the team together of those who already want progress. We have the means, potentially, to create a better way of living, very soon. And it's going to take a lot of work to make that thing happen. That's all. That's our best shot.

I'm confident that what man is capable of doing, in terms of science, in terms of the understanding of mankind himself, in terms of coming to understand what the

Creative Commons

A Ukrainian tank in the Debaltseve area, February 2015

Solar System is all about—mankind has those powers. Mankind has developed those powers. We can develop them. But it's difficult to educate people if the teachers aren't there. Or if you have fake teachers there; then the students are helpless. If the social life in cities and other communities is degenerating, it's very difficult to maintain a civilization.

But what we *must* do, if we're human, really human, we must be devoted to doing the things that would bring that kind of progress into being. That's what I've been doing most of my life. And I can tell you, from my experience, it works. We just don't have enough people doing it right now.

The Case of Ukraine

Q: Good evening. My name is S——. I'm calling from Queens, N.Y., and I'm a Russian-American from St. Petersburg. And this question relates to Ukraine and the events around it. Mr. LaRouche, I do respect you in many ways, and I agree with your economic assessment of the U.S.—cultural, educational, etc. Conceptually, I think we understand what needs to be done, in terms of science and policy.

Now, we understand that there are facts that are available to anyone, including video footage of what's going on in Ukraine, shelling of civilians, the use of Nazis—which is being covered up—and considering the facts of the U.S. toppling governments, creating chaos and sponsoring radicals globally, which are in fact illegal, as far as I understand. What can be done to stop this mob mentality? Practical, realistic, effective steps, which will definitely achieve results. Eliminating the model of perpetual war, so that no one can take over and continue the legacy.

LaRouche: We're coming to a point, right now, at which the decisions to be made that will secure the future of mankind, as opposed to the continued destruction of mankind, are now on the table. Take the case of Ukraine.

Now, I have some intimate, fairly intimate, connections to people in Ukraine. I also have quite a bit of history in terms of Russian history, modern Russian history, especially. I know what's happening. You know probably, as well as I do, that the Ukrainians are not what they are presented to be by the Ukrainian government. And I know people personally, leading people of Ukraine, who agree totally with that.

We have a bunch of Nazis, and they were actually Nazis, on the record, during the Hitler period. These Nazis are running Ukraine today. How? Under the direction of the British Empire—that is, the British monarchy—and other forces like that. I know exactly how it's being done.

Now, the problem is this. Look at what Putin said, for a moment. What is Putin doing? Well, on the one hand, he's doing everything possible to avoid a general thermonuclear war. He probably is doing almost as much, or more, than anybody on this planet, to try to prevent thermonuclear war. Because thermonuclear war, if it were to occur—and there is no such thing as non-thermonuclear war, particularly in this kind of warfare. You have to use those weapons, those kinds of weapons, or you lose the war. Unless you can stop the war.

And to do that, you have to get rid of the Nazis. And you know—I think you do know, from your experience—that Ukraine is now under the control of a bunch of Nazis. That doesn't mean the Ukrainians are Nazis. It means they're intimidated into playing a role, or trying to survive, despite the fact that the government of the United States, among others, under the current President of the United States, is promoting a Nazi regime in Ukraine.

And also, similarly, to be realistic, we're at a point where, if Obama stays in the Presidency for much

kremlin.ru

"President Putin is probably doing almost as much, or more, than anybody on this planet, to try to prevent thermonuclear war."—Lyndon LaRouche (Here, Putin center, with Chinese President Xi Jinping, to his far left, at the May 8, 2015 parade marking the 70th anniversary of Victory in Europe in World War II.)

longer, you're going to have a thermonuclear war, and there won't be any civilization coming out of it. So, getting rid of Obama, getting him out of there, and getting people like him, even getting the British Empire out of there, is absolutely essential. Because the rest of the world, which is being more and more influenced by the BRICS movement, as in China, as in India, as in some nations of South America—the movements there are the kind of movements which are needed in order to build a decent condition of life for humanity.

And I am sure—I've studied it well enough to know—that Putin is actually trying to do a very good job, with good intentions.

But how can he express those good intentions, when the British Empire, of the Queen and company, as well as the Nazis, are now controlling Ukraine? How can we have peace? We have an Obama who wants to make world war. How can we have peace? And therefore, this depends upon the intellect of people: to understand that there are certain missions which the present age, the present generation, must complete in order to ensure the survival of humanity for the future.

What Is Our Plan?

Q: Hi, this is S— in Orange, Southern California. This whole thing we're discussing is very hard to grasp, but let me just ask a few questions. You know, I'm a ex-engineer, and I worked in strategic planning in my day. My question is: What is the plan?

When we worked in business, we had a strategic plan, and we had an operating plan. The strategic plan is what we wanted for the long-term; the operating plan is what are we going to do this coming year; who's going to do it, what are the goals, what are your checklists, and let's identify people that are going to carry it out. Now, I don't know if we have anything like that. If O'Malley's our man, is he

YouTube

The Denver Marijuana Festival, 2014

going to take a month to sit down and figure this out, and come up with something? I don't ever hear anybody come up with a coherent plan. So how do we get this plan, and how do we...?

LaRouche: Well, we do have some people who do have some good planning. But, when it comes to the present system of the present Presidency... And you know, you go back: Bill Clinton wasn't too bad, you know. He was stuck with a lot of handicaps, and I know him, very well. We have had other Presidents, who I've known, or been associated with, and they were good guys, but, what happened was, the Bushes got in there. The general history of the modern 20th Century in the United States—it's had too many Bushes there. Bushes that you would like to burn, so to speak. Prescott Bush was practically a Nazi, himself. His sons were trained to think like Nazis, or sloppy Nazis, or weak-brained Nazis, huh? We're getting more of that! Obama's a mental case. This guy is *not* fit to be President. Why is he there? Because the British Empire put him there! And we let it happen.

So, the point is coming now, that the issue before us is that the enemies of mankind, the enemies of human culture, the enemies of progress, are now at the terminal end of their ability to control the planet. And they are now determined to stay alive, so they can control the planet. How do they do that? By killing people.

What you've got right now—let's take the case of California. What's the policy of the current governor of California, in direct contrast to his father? The present

one is a killer. What's his policy? Reduce the population of California. That means *mass murder* of the population of California. Well, they say there's a water shortage. Then why is the current governor trying to kill people? His policy is killing people. He's not limiting it to California. He's got neighboring states there. You've got some people in Texas, who are thinking in a similar direction. We also have a policy of a President, who works in the same direction—Obama! Now, what are you complaining about? If you're not complaining about what I'm complaining about, what are you complaining about?

We're at a point that we have to fight our way through, to save this nation. It doesn't mean going to a bloody war; it means trying to avoid all kinds of warfare—but it means going to higher levels of technology. But I can tell you one thing probably most of you don't know. I'm an old enough man to be able to say that. Since the beginning of the 20th Century, with the beginning of the 20th Century, in the United States and Europe, the civilization that had been achieved, over the course of the 19th Century, with all the problems that existed in those periods, was better, in direction, than we've had in the 20th Century, of the 21st Century, presently.

Why? Well, I think there was one genius, one and only one true genius in physical science during the 20th Century. His name was Albert Einstein. And everybody else, who pretended to be a great scientist was a failure. And, if you look at the history of the United States, over the period of the 20th Century, what we have been doing is, we have been degenerating. Oh, we've made some accomplishments, we've done some things. We've built some nice machines, but something in the process was going on, a direction of development. While we were doing the good things—and some of us *were* doing good things—the other guys were destroying everything for which we were working.

So the time has come, in which you have to realize, that mankind *does* deserve a good future. But sometimes, if you want to have a good future, you have to fight for it.

The 20th Century Has Been a Failure

Q: Hi, this is S— from New York. My question for Lyn, is, should we get any sensible candidate for Presidency, how do we insure that that candidate won't be a target of the British Empire, for assassination, as so many of the other past Presidents?

LaRouche: I'm not too much afraid of the old stuff, I think that the old stuff that we've talked about in the past—that's all worn out anyway. You have to realize that we've come to a point, at this point in the 21st Century, where all the things that were done, in a recollection, of the 20th Century, into the 21st, have been a failure. What the problem has been, therefore, is that mankind has, people in general, have lost all confidence in the future.

That's why you're seeing the kind of drug addictions you're seeing. The kind of obscene behavior, which is common among our young people. Degeneration. Why? Why are the young people becoming degenerate? They don't have to be, do they? Well, maybe something compels them to do that. The point is, they're trying to fit in to evil. The smoking habits, the drug habits, that kind of stuff. It's destroying people. Destroying the people, that are doing it to themselves. They're destroying the idea of a future with children, real children. They've become almost cannibals.

And the problem is that we, who are supposed to be the leaders of society, have, in the large degree, failed. Because we went along with the Bushes, instead of the great Presidents, like the Kennedys, or Franklin Roosevelt, before that. What did they do? Well, I think Roosevelt died of old age, and work. The Kennedys were murdered. Nobody was going to wait around for them to be successful. And, you look at the Presidencies—look at the number of Presidents who were actually, really, bums, degenerates: The Bushes were all de-

generates. All Bush Presidencies have been degenerates. Obama is a degenerate. He represents the principle of degeneracy. He's a British stooge.

And therefore, we've got to take the score, properly. The problem is that we allowed, in the 20th Century, with the turn from the century before that, into the 20th Century, the United States, and other nations, to go into a general direction of moral, economic decline. Cultural decline. And the entry beyond that, into the new century: The rate of degeneration has greatly accelerated. So, you want to say, "What's the problem?" The problem is, the people who are running society. How do we cure that? Replace the people who shouldn't be running society. Like Obama.

And, I think the case of O'Malley—O'Malley does typify a prototype of a Presidential candidate, who could possibly turn out to be the President who turned things around, back to the way they're supposed to go.

Glass-Steagall and the Presidency

Q: This is J— from Michigan, and talking about the four-point program that you've come up with, starting with Glass-Steagall, and bringing policies into play for moving on to increase the productive powers of labor, I see it as a problem for all strata of the population, from the general labor, right up to the people who would be the scientists. And I'd like you to comment on how we could overhaul our education program so that we could achieve that goal of increasing the productive powers of labor. And secondarily, would you agree that we should go into—like Roosevelt did, beginning of 1942—where we had price controls introduced to stop speculation?

Would you comment, please?

LaRouche: Yeah, sure! Well, Franklin Roosevelt was actually one of the greatest Presidents we ever had! Here's a guy—he had this disease; he was barely able to even live; he fought like the devil through a whole decade, the better part of a decade, and he became the greatest President who we've had in all modern times! And, he died of exhaustion! And he partly died of exhaustion because of what he was working against.

I used to have an association with some people who were working with Franklin Roosevelt. I wasn't of any significance at that time, but I had contact with people who were in that position, of leaders in fighting the war, for example, and so forth. And, what happened is, by a process of assassinating Presidents, and doing all kinds of evil things, which are done by the "financial interests," shall we shall call them, we destroyed what we had actually made through the aid of Franklin Roosevelt.

And you had the Kennedy brothers, they were both very positive elements. You had other people who were more or less positive elements; you had some people in the 1980s—some of them had some positive elements, but they tended to get shot by assassination attempts, and things like that.

And, then what I saw later in the process: I saw Bill Clinton come into power, I saw him in a crippled role—I don't think he was a crippled person—but, he was in a crippled role, as the President at that time. And the British got rid of him! The British destroyed him. They set the whole thing up! I was involved personally in dealing with that. I was associated with him in that way. And, actually, despite the fact that we never got to meet directly, we were always in touch indirectly. And, I can tell you, this guy would've saved the nation if he hadn't been trapped. He was trapped. He was trapped by whom? By the British queen. It was Queen Elizabeth II, who did the job to sink Bill, to discredit him.

And what do we get for letting him be discredited? You got *Bushes . . . more Bushes*! What have you gotten since then? And if you like it, you're insane!

Q: This is T— in Northern California. The question that I have for Lyn—thank you for being on tonight—the question that I have is, the Trans-Pacific Partnership fast-track thing went through Senate last week, I believe it was. And what can we do to get the House to turn the corner and get the Trans-Pacific Partnership stopped, and get the BRICS substituted?

LaRouche: I think this O'Malley attempt, which has been going on, I guess a couple days from now, right? That attempt I find to be a very credible proposition. In other words, I can't guarantee what he's going to do, what all is going to come. But I say, of all the Presidential types, or proto-types, that I know right now, he would fit the match. How he would go from there, I don't know.

But there's also another consideration: That there's no such thing as a President, who, by himself, makes a good Presidency. Any good Presidency in the United

Albert Einstein

States, involves a joint grouping; people who share a common mission.

Now how does it work? Well, you get a President in there, he's accepted; once he's accepted (you're not quite sure yet), but when he's accepted, and you see him doing what he promised to do, or is committed to doing, then you begin to see a Presidency emerging, with the teamwork among the people responsible. You see this in the history of the United States, all over the place. Then, you find you've got a President.

Why is the President so important? Is he some miracle man, or something? No, it's not that. He represents a team of people, *who have a destiny in their eyes*, looking out at the world. And that destiny increases and develops, as it did with Franklin Roosevelt. And that produces something, which makes for a great nation: the United States! As Franklin Roosevelt did.

And some of the people who were assassinated; assassinated by whom? Well, key figures of the United States did that! They assassinate Presidents, you know! How did you get rid of a President you don't like? You get somebody to assassinate him, and we know who the assassin types are! We know the record.

And, so therefore, the question is, we have to understand that it's our responsibility, as individual human beings. If we can grow up to understand what this whole business is all about, as I do, then you can bring people together to cooperate, to create a true Presidential team. And this is not by magic; this is a process, a social process. And if it works, if the team works, then you're probably going to get a good Presidency. It may not be the perfect one, but it's a good one, and the best thing you can do is get a good one, if you can't get anything better.

The Genius of Vernadsky...

Q: This is E— from Wilmington, Del. My question to you, Mr. LaRouche, is, well, you made this provocative statement about Albert Einstein being the only competent scientist in the 20th Century, and I'm not disagreeing with this, but I'm just saying, wouldn't you have also wanted to add, notwithstanding Vernadsky? And I want to see you make a comment on how Vernadsky sizes up in your estimation.

LaRouche: Well, Vernadsky, of course, is a different person. Vernadsky is a genius, a true genius. He was the first one to actually define, systematically, what the practical distinction is of man from beast. Because just think about it. What's the difference between an animal and a human being? Now, some people get confused on this thing. The difference is that the animals don't do any better than they're taught to do. Maybe experience teaches it to them. But they don't create a species, a form of species, which is superior to what the species had been before.

And so, he understood that principle, and he understood a lot of derivatives and benefits from that insight that he had. But he was one of the greatest geniuses that we have in modern times, particularly in his generation. And people still today, as I do sometimes, have wondered how this guy happened to become such a genius. Because of a lot of the kinds of things he discovered, as opposed to all the other kinds of people who didn't do that sort of thing.

No, there's no question about that. Vernadsky is one of the great geniuses of modern history. And his achievements, insofar as they were achievements, have been remarkable. It's unusual, absolutely unusual. No, he's a man I've learned a great deal from.

...And Furtwängler

Q: This is W— from Virginia. Mr. LaRouche, I read the transcript on the discussion you had, on what really is music, and I've also had a CD of Schubert's 9th Symphony, conducted by Wilhelm Furtwängler for a long time. I've listened to it; I really enjoy it. I'm not a music student, and I'm not an expert in Classical culture, so I just wonder if you could do us a favor, and specify the importance of Classical music.

LaRouche: All right. Classical music is sometimes over-rated by looking at it the wrong way. What happens is, you have to look at mankind as such, as a species. Because no animal can do what mankind does, and Classical music expresses, in its true expression, precisely that kind of feature.

Furtwängler particularly—he's the greatest composer who survived into the 20th Century. Furtwängler's understanding—it was something absolutely known. Brahms was dead; the greatest composers of the earlier period were deceased, and here comes along Furtwängler, who, of course, has quite a family background, to add to his knowledge and his accomplishments. And what he did in the few parts of the decades that he lived, is itself remarkable. This man was a true genius. And his famous 9th Symphony of Schubert is, as presented by him, is a real jewel. It's absolutely unique.

What that means is not that he was the greatest genius of that period, in music, but the fact was that there were so few who were able to approach the level he had achieved. And this reflected an effect of a degeneration in music, and in the quality of musicians. Their ability wasn't bad; many were bad, but they weren't necessarily bad ones. But he had a special capability of doing things that had not been done.

He was a continuation of something like Brahms and Mozart and so forth. It was a continuation of something great. And he represented, essentially, with a few friends of mine, who were great musicians, he represented a quality of achievement which is relatively unique. And the great suffering I feel, in my experience of music, in particular, is that we didn't get good musicians. Oh, we got people who had competence, yes. But I'm talking about composers, real composers, ones who create a mark ahead of anything that had ever been done before.

That's what I like. That's what I would really emphasize.

So, the point is, the history is, that mankind, when mankind is developing, whether in music or other departments of human achievement, the name for mankind's purpose in life is achievement. It's growth. Growth of mankind. Mankind's rising to a higher level than had been achieved before. And mankind rejoices when somebody in mankind comes up, and achieves something which others wish they could have done, but on the other hand, they rejoice in the fact that it happened.

www.ingramcontent.com/pod-product-compliance
Lightning Source LLC
Chambersburg PA
CBHW060837290526
45792CB00006BB/1958